Assembly Lan
Coding in C

ARM and NEON

Robert Dunne

Assembly Language Coding in Color: ARM and NEON

Cover Design: Daniel van Loon

ISBN 978-0-970112446 (paperback)

ISBN 978-0-970112439 (digital)

This book refers to and uses the GNU software and Linux kernel. See the GNU General Public License for details which is available from the Free Software Foundation, Inc., Boston, Massachusetts.

Assembly Language Coding in Color: ARM and NEON is an independent publication and has not been authorized, sponsored, or endorsed by any of the hardware or software rights holders described herein.

18 17 16 15 14 13 12 11 10 9 8 7 6 5 4 3 2

Contents

Preface

Assembly language is the computer programming language closest to a CPU's (Central Processing Unit) "machine language." Learning to program in assembly language is an excellent hands-on introduction to computer architecture. However, assembly language has a bad reputation of being difficult to learn. After having taught college courses for over ten years, presented at international conferences for over twenty years, and even taught children's gifted education courses, I've learned that people have many different learning styles and objectives. This book is shorter and is more colorful than than typical textbooks used in a course on assembly language or computer architecture.

Is a book in color worth twice the print production costs of one in black and white? It is for those students struggling to get a working knowledge of a subject where they need to connect concepts to implementation. Learning computer architecture through hands-on assembly language programming experience helps develop well-rounded programmers and computer engineers.

- This tutorial introduces the novice to the basics of the ARM and NEON architectures.
- Although the Raspberry Pi and BeagleBone Black computers are ideal platforms for this book, most other Linux-based ARM systems are also compatible.
- Programmers learn by example and develop their skills by examining and modifying working programs. The sample programs in this book, ranging from five to over one hundred lines of code, are available for download through GitHub.
- Many assembly language books present CPU instructions in "catalog form" along with snippets of coding examples. In this book, CPU instructions are introduced as needed to achieve programming goals as the projects in each chapter progress to the next.
- Over fifty color illustrations are included to explain programming techniques as well as ARM and NEON instructions.
- Programming examples and flow diagrams are color coded to help "connect" concepts to implementation.
- Topics like binary and hexadecimal are introduced through programming examples as well as appearing in appendices.
- The examples in this book have been "classroom tested" with students having very little, if any, previous programming experience. The information is complete, allowing it to be used as an independent study.

Audience for This Book

The goal of this book is to assist students and computer enthusiasts to get on a solid path to understanding computer architecture. It is for those who may have struggled trying to learn assembly language using books that are basically black and white "catalogs of computer hardware instructions." The intended audience is the following:

- Anyone wanting to learn assembly language, especially individuals interested in the Raspberry Pi, the BeagleBone Black, the ARM CPU, and NEON coprocessor architectures in particular.
- Someone who already has assembly language experience, but now wants to become familiar with the ARM CPU and NEON vector coprocessor.
- Students looking for a different approach to become comfortable with CPU architectural concepts and assembly language programming.

Expected prerequisites for someone reading this book to learn assembly language:

- Access to an ARM-based Linux system: Students should be able to get their computers into Linux command line mode. I have included an appendix using the Raspberry Pi as an example that should be adequate for many people needing some assistance.
- No programming experience necessary: Some of my electronics students have limited experience with Basic, C++, Python, or Java, but most have no programming experience.

What's Not in This Book That You May Expect to Find

Preliminary versions of this book have been "field tested" in the classroom by my electronics students. I have specifically targeted this book at those who wanted a different approach to learn computer architecture and assembly language, so it does not contain the following:

- All ARM and NEON instructions: The focus of this book is to get students programming and understanding the architecture as quickly as possible using the most common instructions. Individuals interested in more depth and covering subjects like floating point, software development, and the use of the debugger should consider my other book: *Assembly Language Using the Raspberry Pi: A Hardware Software Bridge*.
- Examples with assembly language with C: Although almost all of the embedded systems I have developed for production "in the real world" are a combination of assembly language with a higher level

Assembly Language Coding in Color

language like C, I decided to only cover that subject briefly in an appendix.

- Electronics interfacing examples: As you might expect in electronics classes, I always have lab exercises that either drive motors or read very sensitive, even micro-volt data. Again, I felt I couldn't properly cover that material in a professional way without almost doubling the size of this book.
- Linux applications development: I use only enough Linux service calls to demonstrate the programming techniques and examples. File I/O, as well as task and thread management, are not included.
- All program code in multiple colors: Color is used to highlight the particular set of instructions and programming techniques being presented at the time. Besides, a full-color 100-line program just looks like too much of a good thing,

Book Organization

The objective is to use hands-on programming examples to reinforce computer architecture concepts.

- The first chapter introduces the concepts and structure of CPU machine code through examples modeled as a calculator.
- A program named "model" is begun in Chapter 2 to demonstrate the work flow of using an editor, assembler, and linker to build and then test an assembly language program. Although it starts as a 5-line program, it will be modified in subsequent chapters until it becomes a 188-line program in Chapter 7.
- Chapter 3 enhances the "model" program with a read/write user interface and includes programming techniques such as nested loops.
- Chapter 4 improves the same program using subroutines and macros, and divides it into multiple source code files.
- Two more subroutines are added in Chapter 5, which use logical and shift instructions to code an application using ASCII, binary, and hexadecimal outputs.
- Chapter 6 illustrates the ARM machine code format and improves the "model" program with data processing instructions using four registers.
- A new subroutine is developed in Chapter 7 that uses indirect, pre-indexed, and post-indexed memory references to modify the "model" program for a final time. A program named "vector" is started which introduces block transfer instructions accessing multiple registers.
- Chapter 8 enhances the "vector" program with NEON coprocessor instructions providing examples of simultaneous operations being performed on logical and integer data and demonstrates interleaved

data storage techniques as well.
- Eight appendices present background information on using editors, setting up the Raspberry Pi, binary, hexadecimal, Linux service calls, and an interface to the C programming language.

About the Author

Robert Dunne has over 40 years of computer experience ranging from developing custom hardware interfaces on supercomputers to teaching technology courses in middle-school gifted-education programs. Starting out with degrees in physics and computer science, he was on staff at a national laboratory and a major engineering firm for ten years before becoming an entrepreneur in the development of embedded systems. He has written well over 100,000 lines of assembler code developing systems and applications on ten unique CPU architectures encompassing mainframes, minicomputers, and microcomputers.

During the past ten years, he has taught three undergraduate courses per semester in digital electronics and embedded systems and is notorious for getting his students working on a lab project within the first 60 seconds of the very first class meeting.

— 1 —
The Calculator

When I ask my students when do they think the first computers were developed, I usually get answers like the 1980s or even the 1940s. Very few know that the basic architecture of almost all computers used in the past 50 years dates back to the 1830s with Charles Babbage's Analytical Engine.

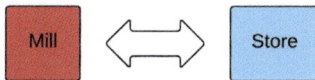

Figure 1.1: Babbage's Analytical Engine

Babbage's Analytical Engine consisted of two principal components:

- Mill: The hardware that did the work (arithmetic and logic operations)
- Store: Location for data storage of intermediate results

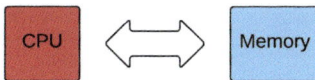

Figure 1.2: "Modern" computer hardware nomenclature

Babbage's mill and store correspond to today's computers:

- CPU (Central Processing Unit): The hardware that does the work (arithmetic and logic operations)
- Memory: Location for data storage of intermediate results

By no means am I implying there existed a positive progression of concepts and devices from Babbage's day to today. The computer pioneers in the 1940s recreated much of what was lost for nearly one hundred years. I personally observed the microcomputer software industry in the 1980s recreate the same mistakes and going down the same wrong paths as the mainframe developers did in the 1960s.

The Machine and Its Language

"Machine Language" generally refers to the numeric codes that instruct the CPU as to which operation is to be performed and on what values.

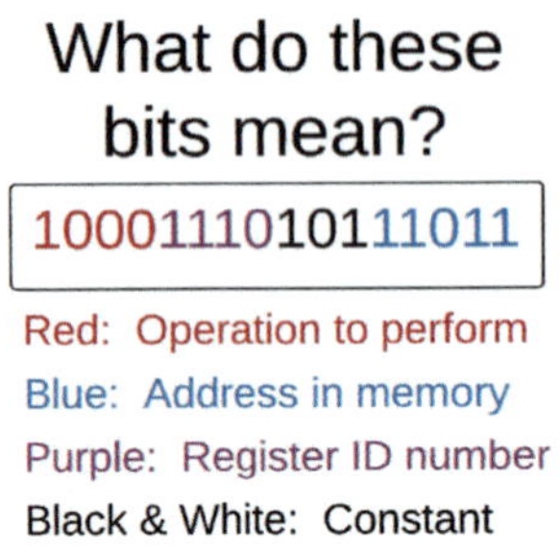

What do these bits mean?

1000111010111011

Red: Operation to perform
Blue: Address in memory
Purple: Register ID number
Black & White: Constant

Figure 1.3: Machine language instruction

An instruction for today's CPUs in machine language is "simply" a package of groups of bits (binary digits, ones and zeros). How does the CPU "know" how to decode each of these machine code instructions? The CPU identifies each component by its bit position in each instruction type. For the benefit of us humans and to provide insight into understanding, I will be color-coding the various parts within the instructions.

I could have chosen any arbitrary mapping of colors to relate to each of the various parts within an instruction, or like almost all books on assembly language, simply stayed with black and white. I could have chosen a mapping that would be the most pleasing from an artistic standpoint, but instead I tried to map what is commonly referred to as the psychological or "emotional meaning" of color to various parts of assembly language and machine codes. I know these meanings are somewhat nebulous and not culturally universal, but I was surprised how close I could get to associating colors with components of CPU instructions.

Red: Operations

The color red is often associated with energy, action, and work. The main reason for having a computer is the "data processing" instructions which obviously include operations like addition and multiplication, but also instructions for moving data. I will be color-coding the operator portion of each instruction in red to identify it as the source of action to be performed.

Blue: Memory

The color blue conjures feelings of depth, security, trust, and wisdom. Today's computer memories are extremely reliable and store trillions of numbers, providing a trusted location to store a huge amount of data. The part of an instruction that points to where the data is located in memory will be coded in blue.

Purple: Registers

Purple has historically been associated with rare and high-quality items. CPUs contain a small amount of very high performance memory called registers. Depending upon the particular CPU design, the number of registers varies from about five up to nearly one hundred. Some of the registers are accessible to user programs in assembly language, and some registers are only accessed by the CPU's electronics to perform its many tasks. The metaphor of coloring these registers purple is enhanced because not only are registers rare and of high-quality, but they are memory (blue) located within the CPU (red), combined to make purple.

Black and White: Constants

The expression "in black and white" often implies a standard or foundation such as a legal contract. Computer programs contain many variables that are continuously changing in registers and memory, but there are also many constants that never change. I will indicate constants with black digits and letters on a white background, a symbol of purity, things that have not been changed or blemished.

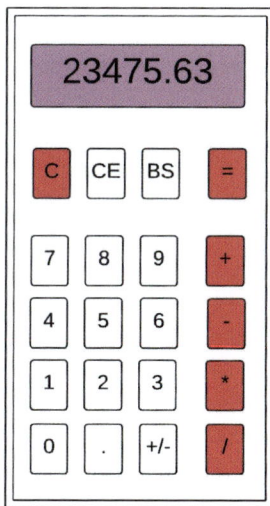

Figure 1.4: Simple calculator model

In order to understand machine language, think of a calculator which has the following features:

- **Display:** Current number being entered or current result of operations
- **Operations:** Clear (C), add(+), subtract(-), multiply(*), divide(/), display(=)
- **Data input:** Digits and decimal point, sign(+/-), clear entry (CE), back space (BS)

When we use a simple calculator, there is a symbiotic partnership to achieve the final calculation: The calculator does the work, and we provide the directions.

The number keys in Figure 1.4 are black digits on a white background. They represent pure numbers, i.e. constants to be entered. The operations to be performed are in red, and the display is in purple. The principal data register in a CPU is generally referred to as the "accumulator." In this calculator example, the accumulator value can be a "running total" or accumulated total that is shown in the display, so I color-coded it as purple, since it's a register.

As an example, we can enter the following sequence of instructions to perform the calculation $13 \times 21 + 6$:

1. **Clear**
2. **Add 13**
3. **Multiply 21**
4. **Add 6**
5. **Display**

Most of the logical and arithmetic operations performed by CPUs are binary operations. Two numbers (called operands) are added, or two operands are multiplied, or one operand is subtracted from another. In our calculator example, the first operand is the value in the display (i.e., the accumulator register), and the second operand is the number being entered.

Op-codes

Although a CPU could be constructed to work with the character string names of operations like clear, add, and multiply, it would be somewhat inefficient. Instead, the CPU designers assign an operation code (op-code) to represent each of the available CPU operations. For example, let the following six numbers be assigned to the following six calculator operations:

1. **Clear (C)**: Load zero into the accumulator.
2. **Add (+)**: Add the value of the operand (being entered) to the current accumulator contents.
3. **Subtract (-)**: Subtract the value of the operand (being entered) from the current accumulator contents.
4. **Multiply (*)**: Multiply the value of the operand (being entered) to the current accumulator contents.
5. **Divide (/)**: Divide the current contents of the accumulator by the operand (being entered).
6. **Display (=)**: Copy the current contents of the accumulator to the display line.

Assembly Language Coding in Color

If we use the above numeric assignments to translate our previous sequence of instructions to calculate 13×21+6, we will get the following machine code:

Step number	Operation		Op-code with operand
1	Clear	translates to	1 : 0
2	Add 13	translates to	2 : 13
3	Multiply 21	translates to	4 : 21
4	Add 6	translates to	2 : 6
5	Display	translates to	6 : 0

Table 1.1: Translate "assembly code" into "machine code."

Note that in this simple model of a calculator being used as a computer, I've represented each instruction as a binomial: an op-code and operand pair. In Table 1.1's translation to machine code, binary operations like Add and Multiply are converted to form "op-code : operand" pairs. Unitary operations, such as Clear and Display, are converted to the form "op-code : 0" because there was no operand. So in this example, we would calculate 13×21+6 by entering "Clear, Add 13, Multiply 21, Add 6, Display" on a calculator, but the corresponding computer program (in machine language) would be the sequence "1 : 0, 2 : 13, 4 : 21, 2 : 6, 6 : 0."

Memory

What about the other half of Babbage's computer: the "store" ("memory" in today's terminology)? Babbage needed memory for the storage of intermediate results and so do we. In an arithmetic problem like 13×14+15×16, we can't just multiply 13 times 14, add 15, and then multiply by 16. The answer would be wrong because by convention, multiplication has precedence over addition: the 15 and 16 have to be multiplied before being added to the product of 13 and 14. There is an implied parenthesis in this calculation as follows: (13×14)+(15×16). With our non-memory calculator, we would have to write down the intermediate value of 13×14 and then reenter it after we calculate 15×16. Memory calculators do this "writing down" and reentering for us.

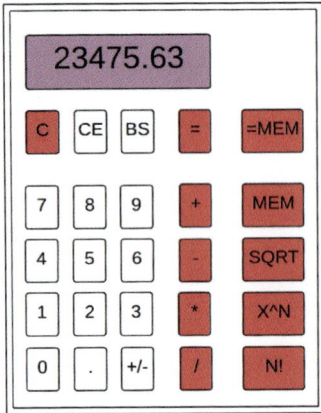

Figure 1.5: Memory Calculator with functions

In our calculator model shown in Figure 1.5, we have more operations, two of which are related to memory: Store (=MEM) and Load (MEM). Since we added two more operations to the calculator, we must also add two more op-codes: Store (op-code = 7) and Load (op-code = 8).

Op-codes 1 through 8 are defined as follows:

1. **Clear (C)**
2. **Add (+)**
3. **Subtract (-)**
4. **Multiply (*)**
5. **Divide (/)**
6. **Display (=)**
7. **Store (=MEM)**: Copy the contents of the accumulator into a memory location.
8. **Load (MEM)**: Copy the contents of a memory location into the accumulator.

Is this the best approach for using memory? The above Store command is fine, but the Load instruction is too limiting. In some simple memory calculators that store only one value in memory, there is an "Add memory" command, but what if you want to multiply using the value in memory or divide by it? What we really would like to do is to not just reload a saved value, but use it in any of the previously defined operations such as Add or Multiply.

Most CPU implementations include a "flag" in the instruction that indicates if the operand is immediate (value is in the operand itself) or is from memory. In my color-coding scheme, immediate flags will be blue because they help point to where the data is located, in memory or in the instruction. Our binomial instruction format (op-code and operand) now becomes a trinomial (op-code, immediate-flag, and operand). If we use the above operations including the new immediate flag to write a little program to calculate $13 \times 14 + 15 \times 16$, we will get the following code:

Assembly Language Coding in Color

Step number	Operation		Op-code :i- flag : operand
1	Clear	translates to	1 : 1 : 0
2	Add 13	translates to	2 : 1 : 13
3	Multiply 14	translates to	4 : 1 : 14
4	Store Mem 0	translates to	7 : 0 : 0
5	Clear	translates to	1 : 1 : 0
6	Add 15	translates to	2 : 1 : 15
7	Multiply 16	translates to	4 : 1 : 16
8	Add Mem 0	translates to	2 : 0 : 0
9	Display	translates to	6 : 1 : 0

Table 1.2: Translate "assembly code" into "machine code."

The above system actually works fine, but can we improve on the performance? Storing intermediate results into memory always takes time. An accumulator is also memory, but it's very fast local memory inside the CPU, and we can also use it as an operand in our instructions. Although some CPUs have only one accumulator, the vast majority have several. The ARM has 16 user accessible general purpose registers, most of which can be used as accumulators for making calculations.

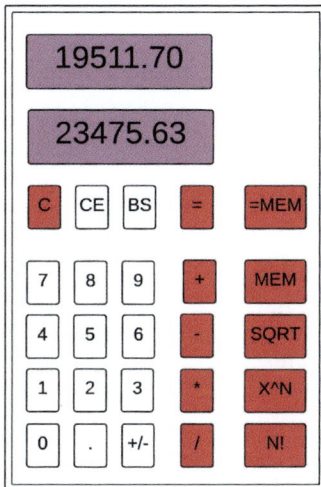

Figure 1.6: Two-accumulator Calculator

Let's expand our calculator model to have two accumulators and see how that changes our assembly language. First, our instructions are no longer trinomials consisting of three numbers, but now have a fourth component: we have to specify which accumulator is being used in the operation. In the previous one-accumulator calculator model, we only had one accumulator, so it was the only one that could be used and therefore did not need to be specified.

Step number	Operation		Op-code : acc : i-flag : operand
1	Clear A0	translates to	1 : 0 : 1 : 0
2	Add 13 to A0	translates to	2 : 0 : 1 : 13
3	Multiply A0 by 14	translates to	4 : 0 : 1 : 14
4	Clear A1	translates to	1 : 1 : 1 : 0
5	Add 15 to A1	translates to	2 : 1 : 1 : 15
6	Multiply A1 by 16	translates to	4 : 1 : 1 : 16
7	Add A1 to A0	translates to	2 : 0 : 0 : 1
8	Display A0	translates to	6 : 0 : 1 : 0

Table 1.3: Use two accumulators: A0 and A1

Assembly Language

A machine language instruction is composed of multiple integer fields indicating which operation is to be performed and on what data. Assembly language substitutes names for these numbers, and generates one machine code instruction for each line of assembly language coding. Almost every assembly language program for all CPUs consists of four columns:

1. Label: Name associated with instruction's memory address
2. Op-code: The operation being performed (add, sub, shift, ...)
3. Operands: Location of the data (usually a register combined with a constant, another register, or memory address)
4. Comment: Describes why the instruction is being used

Each column is separated by one or more blanks or tab characters. How wide is a column? Typical columns are 8 to 10 characters wide with the exception of the rightmost column which contains comments. The assembler doesn't care if it's one blank, two blanks, or more. We line up the columns of assembly code for the ease of reading by the programmers.

```
v_ascz:   push   {R0_R8,LR}    @ Save contents of registers R0 through R8, LR
          sub    R2,R1,#1      @ R2 is index for searching string for null.
hunt4z:   ldrb   R0,[R2,#1]!   @ Load next character from string.
          cmp    R0,#0         @ Set Z status bit if null found
          bne    hunt4z        @ If not null, go examine next character.
          sub    R2,R1         @ Calculate length of message (not counting null)
```

Listing 1.1: Example of assembly language source code

Green: Comments

There is more to a well-written program than the machine code itself. Program design and maintenance requires documentation. "Internal documentation" is the description of the program appearing in the program itself and consists of two types of comments:

1. **Global**: These comments describe what a section of code is doing. They normally consist of more than one line of text and are not on the same physical text lines as the actual machine code instructions. Global comments are used in both assembly language as well as higher level languages.
2. **Local**: These comments share the text line with the actual machine code instructions. They are rarely needed in higher level languages, but are very important in assembly language to explain not what the code is doing but *why* the line of code is doing it.

Importance of comments: They're not necessary for a program to successfully run, and many programmers use very few comments. They're necessary for program maintenance, whether it be by a new programmer next week or by the original programmer a month or even several years later. When I was an undergraduate student and took a course in assembly language programming, my professor thought comments were so important that he subtracted one letter grade for each line of code that didn't have a local comment. That was a bit extreme, but I got the point. I confess that in my production code I don't comment every line, but I do comment much more than others. In this book, I will be commenting on almost every line to help set an example as well as explain what's going on in the code.

I assigned the color green to comments for two reasons:

1. Green represents nature, harmony, safety, and balance. Comments provide these attributes to a computer program.
2. Several editors that I have used for either program development or hardware development display comments in green.

The following excerpt from an assembly language program shows both global (lines 3 through 7) and local comments. There are almost as many ways to mark the beginning of a comment as there are programming languages. In this book, I will be using the @ (at-sign) which is commonly used with the GNU "as" assembler that comes standard with most Linux distributions. In other assemblers, both for the ARM as well as other CPUs, the semicolon is commonly used to indicate the beginning of a comment. The comment ends at the end of line.

   In other assemblers for the ARM as well as the GNU assembler for other CPUs (such as the x86), the comment indicator is #, /, or semicolon. In other computer languages, comments are indicated by <!, //*, // - -, #, C, and even REM. The GNU "as" assembler also supports using /* to begin a comment with an associated */ to end the comment, but I won't be showing that in the examples.

1.	.global	v_ascz	@ External entry location for subroutine v_ascz
2.			
3. @		Subroutine v_ascz will display a string of characters	
4. @		R1: Points to beginning of ASCII string	
5. @		End of string will be marked by a null byte	
6. @		LR: Contains the return address	
7. @		All register contents will be preserved	
8.			
9. v_ascz:	push	{R0_R8,LR}	@ Save registers R0 through R8, LR
10.	sub	R2,R1,#1	@ R2 is index while searching string for null.
11. hunt4z:	ldrb	R0,[R2,#1]!	@ Load next character from string (and increment R2 by 1)
12.	cmp	R0,#0	@ Set Z status bit if null found
13.	bne	hunt4z	@ If not null, go examine next character.
14.	subs	R2,R1	@ Calculate message length (not counting null)
15.	mov	R0,#1	@ Code for stdout (standard output monitor)
16.	mov	R7,#4	@ Service command code to write string.
17.	svcne	0	@ Issue command to display string on stdout
18.			
19.	pop	{R0_R8,LR}	@ Restore saved register contents
20.	bx	LR	@ Return to the calling program
21.	.end		

Listing 1.2: Sample of local and global comments, directives, and conditionals

In Listing 1.2, I've included the line number for each line of the program. These numbers are not actually in the text file itself, but usually provided by the editor and assembler.

Yellow: Decisions

Yellow relates to new ideas, creativity, and critical thinking. The op-codes on lines 13, 14 and 17 of Listing 1.2 have two colors. Many of the ARM assembly language operations (appearing in the second column) are compounds containing both an operation and a condition. In the flowcharts, I will be coding conditions and decisions in yellow, but in the program listings, I will leave them in black because yellow is too hard to see on a white background. It will be "SVCNE" instead of "SVCNE" in all programming examples. Why not simply use

"SVCNE"? I really do want to highlight that these mnemonics are compounds of opcodes with conditions, not simply opcodes by themselves.

Computers are great for doing the same thing over and over again, but on different sets of input data. Sometimes, we write a program to perform the calculations differently, depending on the type and values of the data being processed. Making these decisions, as well as knowing when to exit these repetitive loops are done by branch instructions (a.k.a., jump instructions) and conditional test instructions. We'll examine these branching techniques more in the next section on documentation.

Orange: Directives and Macros

Lines 1 and 21 of Listing 1.2 have "pseudo" operations in their second column. These pseudo-ops do not correspond to a machine code operation, but are commands to the assembler itself. They may generate one machine code instruction like the op-codes do, or they could generate many machine code instructions, or even generate no code at all. I have colored these pseudo-ops orange because they are operations (red) that are new ideas (yellow). There are two types of pseudo-ops in assembly language:

1. Assembler directives: Commands providing a variety of information to the assembler such as where the program starts and ends, generates data, and organizes the program code. These directives, within the "as" assembler, also begin with a period.
2. Macros: These custom commands enable the programmer to define new operations that essentially look equivalent to any of the hardware opcodes such as ADD and SUB. Macros make programming easier, less prone to error, and provide better documentation. Chapter 4 will introduce the use of macros.

In Case It Matters

One of the first questions programmers and hardware developers should ask when beginning a new computer language is, "Is it case sensitive?" In other words, are the commands and variable names, such as "Start, start, stArt, and staRT," all the same to the compiler or is each one unique? In programming languages like C, Java, and Python, as well as the Verilog hardware description language, each "start" in the above list is unique: "Start" is different from "start" which is different from "stArt" which is different from "staRT." In programming languages like Ada, Basic, Fortran, as well as the VHDL hardware description language, all of the above would be considered the same. Most assemblers, including the GNU "as" assembler that we're using, are not case sensitive.

So if case doesn't matter for assembly language, which should you use: add or ADD, mult or MULT, or any other combination? It's primarily your choice and style. From what I've observed, the majority of programmers and hardware developers today, including myself, use lowercase for programming and hardware development. In this book's program listings, I will provide the register names in uppercase and everything else generally in lower case.

Documentation

Program documentation is used during both construction and long term operation of a software application. It tells the development programmers what the application is supposed to do and tells maintenance programmers what the application is doing and how it's doing it.

Some computer languages are somewhat self-documenting. Assembly language is definitely not one of these. One of the first languages developed after assembly language was Cobol which has been present in business applications for over 50 years. Although professionally trained programmers were needed to write Cobol programs, almost anyone who could read English could read the Cobol program instructions and get a very good understanding of what was being done. Even today's commonly used languages like C and Java contain structures like loops and objects which help identify what is being done in the program.

Documentation basically exists at three levels:

1. **Narrative**: A description in words, charts, tables, and examples explaining what the application does. To some degree it even recommends how the application should perform its assigned tasks.
2. **Diagrams**: There has been a variety of graphic modeling languages over the years beginning with traditional flowcharts through the Universal Modeling Language (UML). Their diagrams show program structure and flow.
3. **Internal documentation in the code itself**: All programs should have comments interspersed among lines of code saying what is being done, why it's being done, and how it's being done. For higher level languages like C and Java, internal documentation is important. In assembly language it is crucial.

I never really liked flowcharts. However, many students new to programming say this graphical approach helps them grasp the logic flow more readily. So I'll use them in the first few chapters to explain some programming techniques and even use them to explain how an ARM instruction works. I've seen flowcharts used not only to document software, but also in the automotive, HVAC (heating, air conditioning), and other industries.

I'll be using three basic flowchart symbols (and then three alterations to one of them).

- **Process**: Identifies a task, such as adding three numbers.
- **Decision**: Shows alternate paths the program can take based upon current values in the data.
- **Terminator**: Identifies the beginning and ending points of a portion of the program

Figure 1.7: Basic flowchart symbols

Although I could use the process block throughout, I will also use three other symbols when the process is more specific: preparation, predefined process, and display.

- **Preparation**: A process like initializing a running total to zero (i.e., it is a process, but not the "main act")
- **Predefined Process**: A compound process like taking the square root (normally located external to the current program coding)
- **Display**: A process where the computer user receives a displayed message.

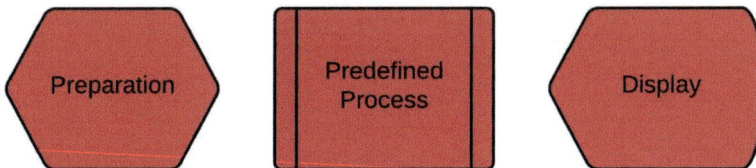

Figure 1.8: Specialized process symbols

Flowcharts containing only comments will be presented in green. Flowcharts containing assembly language instructions will have the following colors:

- **Processes are red**: These boxes show action being performed.
- **Decisions are yellow**: Many different emotions have been assigned to yellow, including creativity and wisdom, which I have assigned to the decision diamonds.
- **Terminators are blue or red**: Programs reside in memory, so I'll usually identify their beginning as blue (a memory location) and their exit as red (an action).

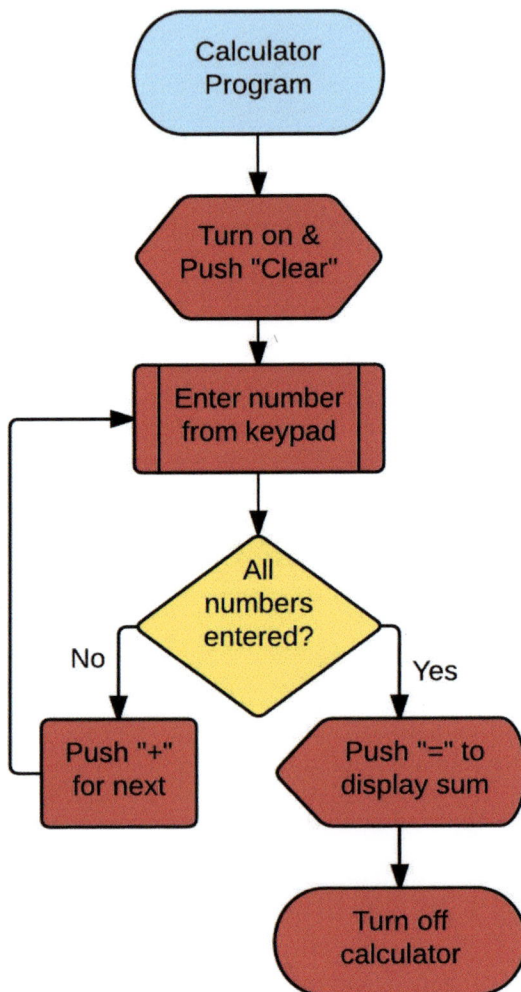

Figure 1.9: Program using predefined process

Assembly Language Coding in Color

Figure 1.9 illustrates a flowchart for a program that calculates the sum of a series of numbers using a calculator. The following steps are performed:

1. Turn on the calculator
2. Push clear to initialize the accumulator and set the display to zero.
3. Enter next number from keypad (This is actually a multi-step procedure where one or more numeric keys are pushed and may include a decimal point.)
4. Test whether the last number of the list has been added.
5. If not, push the "+" sign and then enter the next number in the list.
6. If the last number has been entered, then push the "=" key to display the final result.
7. Turn off the calculator.

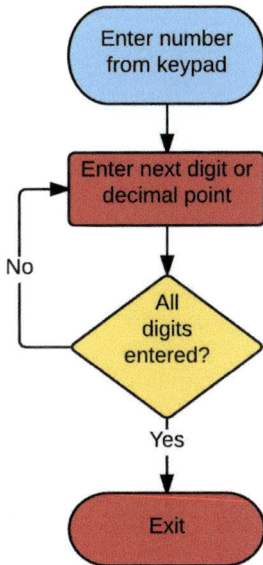

Figure 1.10: Predefined process "Enter number from keyboard"

Figure 1.10 illustrates the "predefined process" of "Enter number from keypad" called from the previous flowchart. Predefined processes, also known as subroutines, procedures, functions, and methods, are common to computer programming languages. Their use provides a structure leading to more reliable as well as more compact code. Most of the programming examples in this book involve building subroutines to perform specific tasks.

Figure 1.11: Connecting
segments of a flowchart

The final flowchart symbol that appears for very large programs is the off-page link. It is used to divide a single flowchart into smaller segments. With a large piece of paper, off-page links would neither be necessary nor used very often. It will not be necessary to use that symbol in this book due to the size of program segments that are being discussed.

Although I think flowcharts are great as an introduction to how machine code instructions work and are to be used, I never really did like flowcharts for documenting program coding. It seemed like it took at least ten times longer to make the flowchart than to write the code. Apparently I'm not alone in that opinion because the traditional flowchart from the 1960s for program documentation has generally died out and been replaced by more practical techniques. The Universal Modeling Language (UML) has been available for many years for documenting software structure (usually for higher level languages) and development on many levels. Its "activity diagram" is the closest thing to traditional flowcharts, and it has some added real-time (i.e., embedded systems) features. Also, pseudo code which uses a somewhat arbitrary program-like verbal description of how the code works is more popular today.

Summary of Color Codes

I've chosen color codes to be associated with computer components and programming due to the following "emotional meanings" of colors:

- CPU operations are red: Energy, action, work
- Memory is blue: Stability, truth, depth, wisdom
- Registers (memory within the CPU) are purple (red + blue): Quality, rare
- Decisions are yellow: Creativity, new ideas, critical thinking
- Directives and macros are orange: Energy and action combined with creativity and new ideas
- Comments are green: Safety, balance, natural

— 2 —
Compile, Link, Execute

From a programmer's perspective, software development is a vicious cycle of modify the program, test the program, modify the program, test the program, modify the program, test the program until we are satisfied with the test results. As described in Chapter 1, an assembly language program consists of lines of text which we will create and modify using a simple text editor. We then test the program by translating it into ARM machine code to be run from the Linux command prompt. In this book, we use the GNU assembler and linker included with most Linux distributions.

Updated source code file

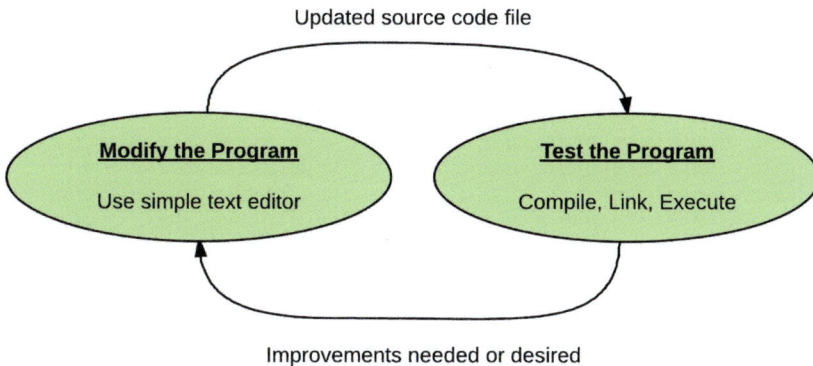

Figure 2.1: Dividing a program into modules

Simple First Program

How does a computer start, run, and stop? The hardware knows where to start the first instruction after power-up or reset, and there is an ARM instruction that effectively halts its execution. Those are controlled by the Linux operating system in the environment in which we're working. Your program starts when Linux gives it control at the "_start" label; and when your program chooses to quit, it will return control back to Linux using a service call (svc 0 instruction). Actually, Linux never gives up full control to your program, but don't be concerned about that for now.

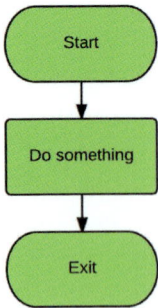

Figure 2.2: Simple
program flow

The flowchart in figure 2.2 illustrates the major flow of a program: It gets CPU control, it does its intended job, and finally it returns control.

The only purpose of the first program (Listing 2.1) is to start and then quit. It "quits" by returning control to Linux using service code 7. Linux provides a variety of services to a running program such as reading and writing disk files, and communicating with keyboards, monitors, and networks.

The ARM CPU has 16 user-accessible general purpose registers: R0 through R15. The contents of register R7 indicates what service is requested. For example, [R7]=3 tells Linux to read from a file or device, [R7]=4 tells Linux to write to a file or device, and [R7]=1 tells Linux that your program is ready to stop running and return full control back to Linux. Other registers provide Linux with additional information such as what data is to be written and which file is to be accessed.

What's the difference between R7 and [R7]? Typically, [R7] means the current contents of register R7, while R7 represents the address of register R7, which is 7 in machine code instructions.

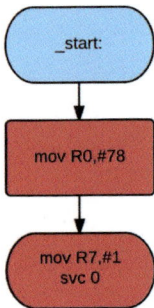

Figure 2.3: Flowchart of
Listing 2.1

When an application terminates, it returns an "exit code" in register R0 to Linux that can be tested in command line scripts. The value of the exit code will be placed into command line variable $? which can be displayed by the "echo $?" command line. Note: Although the exit code can range from 0 through 255, typical values for exit codes are 0 (implying a successful application) and 1 (implying the application somehow failed to perform as expected). Many of the other possible codes are loosely defined depending on application. In this chapter, we will use the full 0 to 255 range, but in real applications, please use only 0, 1, or a few of the other specific "error" code numbers. Check the Internet for sysexits.h in Unix or Linux to get some of these codes.

Assembly Language Coding in Color

```
         .global    _start:     @ Indicate _start is global for linker
_start:  mov        R0,#78      @ Move a decimal 78 value into register R0
         mov        R7,#1       @ Move an integer value of 1 into register 7.
         svc        0           @ Perform service call to Linux
         .end
```

Listing 2.1: Program to set "exit" code

In the above listing, three CPU instructions will be generated: two moves and a service call, all with their op-codes shown in red. For the moves, constants 78 and 1 (shown in black) will be loaded into registers R0 and R7 (purple), respectively. The order of the parameters is similar to that of higher level languages like C and Python. The instruction "MOV R0,#78" means [R0] = 78 where the hash (#) tells the assembler that 78 is an immediate constant contained within the instruction itself. I have colored the hash blue because it points to where the operand is located: either in memory or immediately within the instruction.

The program has two assembler directives, .global and .end shown in orange, These generate no ARM code, but provide information to the assembler. The .global directive tells the assembler to pass the label _start onto the linker, so that Linux will know what memory location (blue) contains the starting location of the program. Although the ".end" directive is not necessary, I find it comforting to know that I didn't lose part of the program in a truncated copy of cut and paste.

Language Interpreter and Compiler

The "human language" source code of our programs must be translated to machine language in order to be executed by the CPU. This translation can be done all at once before any of the machine code is executed or it can be converted and executed line by line as it is needed. The two approaches are the following:

- Interpreter: Translate each line of source code to machine language line by line just before it is executed.
- Compiler: Convert the entire source code file to machine language all at one time.

Assembly language as well as C and Java are almost always compiled. Languages like Basic have traditionally been interpreted. There are merits to each approach which we won't go into here except saying that interpreter code is easier to write and debug, while compiled code offers much higher performance at execution time.

The following four steps will be performed to run each program:

1. **Edit (make the source code):** The source code such as that shown in Listing 2.1 has to be entered (or copied) into a text file. In my classes, I currently recommend using either the leafpad editor or GNU nano editor. They are both included with most Linux distributions and are very easy to use. If you're more comfortable with vi, vim, or emacs, please use it instead. I do. I just want the students to focus on the ARM architecture and assembly language and not be distracted by the complexity of other software. Appendix E will provide some help with editors if needed.

2. **Compile (make the object code):** Each "machine language" instruction executed by the ARM CPU is composed of several fields ("groups of bits"), which could be entered as integers, but would be a lot of work. In assembly language, the fields are entered with mnemonic names and decimal, hexadecimal, or binary numbers. The "as" program, known as a compiler (or assembler in the case for assembly language), converts the text lines to the binary instructions (object code) needed by the ARM CPU and NEON coprocessor.

3. **Link (make the executable program):** The "ld" linker program combines multiple object files into a single executable file.

4. **Execute (run the program):** This step is the objective of the previous three steps, but how do you know if your program is doing what you wanted it to do or is even doing anything at all? You'll need some type of I/O (Input/Output). In this chapter, we'll use the echo command line to assist with a little output, and Chapter 3 will demonstrate input from the keyboard and output to the monitor screen.

The following four GNU/Linux command lines are entered in response to the Linux command line prompt, which I will shorten to just ~$. If your computer is configured to boot straight into the Graphical User Interface (GUI), then you'll have to enter the command line mode from the LXTerminal desktop icon. Yes, there's a way to automate most of these commands, but for now it's good practice to know what's going on: edit, compile, link, execute.

```
~$ nano model.s
~$ as -o model.o model.s
~$ ld -o model model.o
~$ ./model
```

Listing 2.2: GNU and Linux commands to edit, compile, link, and execute

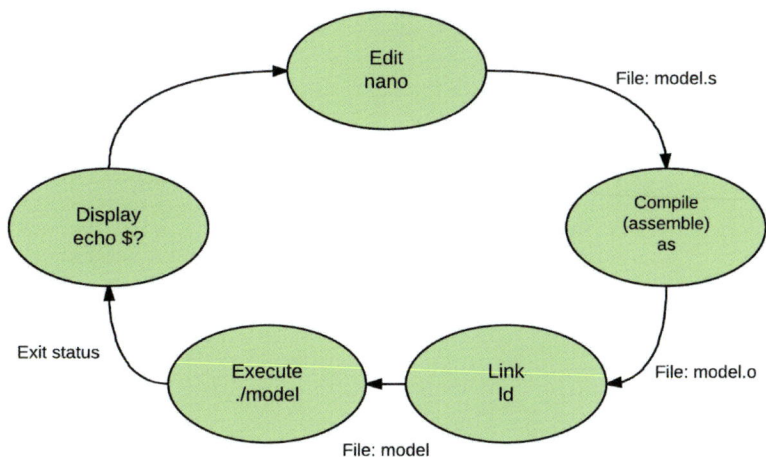

Figure 2.4: Work flow of testing a program update

File names appearing in Figure 2.4 and command line Listing 2.2:

- **model.s:** Source file containing assembly language
- **model.o:** Object file containing ARM and NEON machine code
- **model:** Executable file ready to run on a Linux/ARM based computer system.

Actually any file names could have been chosen: *source1* or *PGM-2* or *mycode*. I chose *model* because I use it in my classes to subtly introduce students to design patterns for software development. Design patterns are very important in the development of large programs and most important to the long-term program maintenance. If you plan to do any serious programming, whether in assembly language or a higher level language, please investigate using design patterns where Model View Controller (MVC) is a classic example.

In the event an error is detected by the "as" assembler command, then you'll have to go back and update the program source code using the nano editor. It is also possible that the linker ("ld" command) will catch some misspellings, and then you'll have to go back to the editor, correct the mistake, then reassemble the program and relink it again. An easy way to provide some relief of re-entering command lines on many Linux systems is to use the up-arrow key which will bring back command lines previously entered.

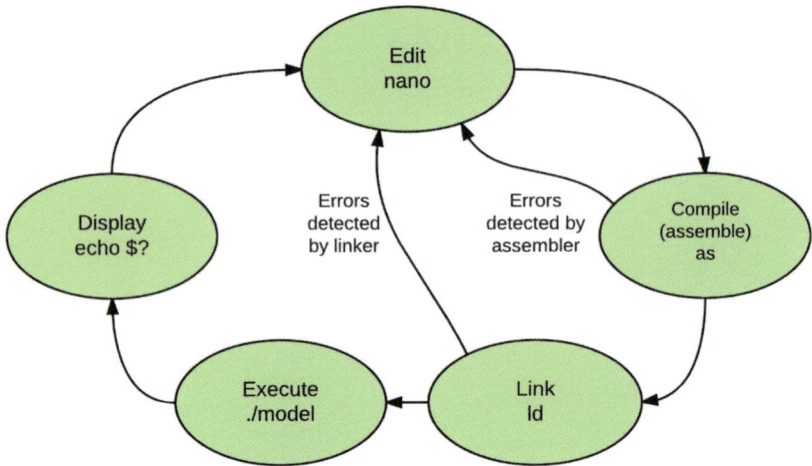

Figure 2.5: Errors found during assembly and linking

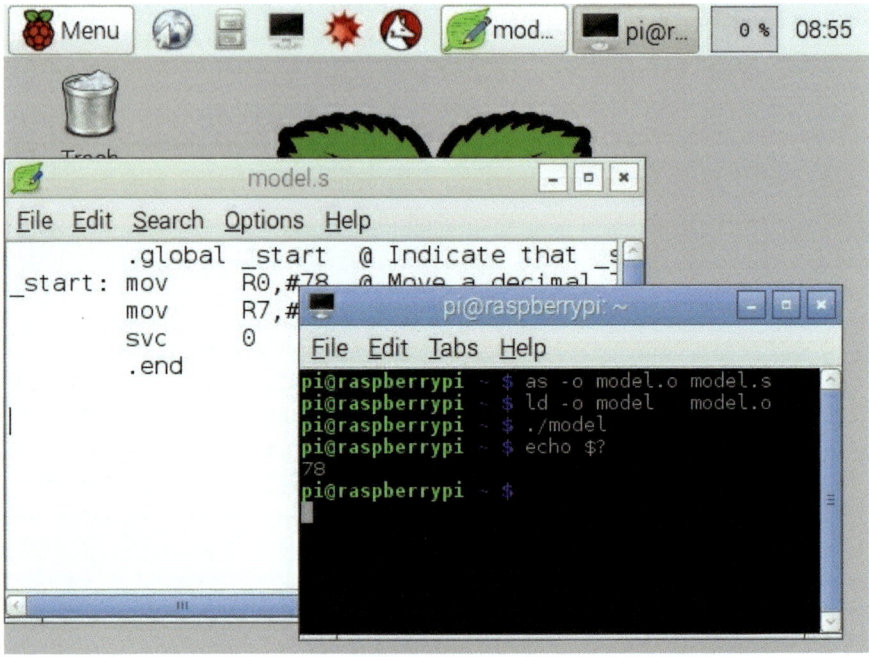

Figure 2.6: Two windows open: one for editing and one for testing

The compiling, linking, and testing must be done from the command prompt, but there are several ways to edit the source code program. Most of my students prefer to work using two open windows in the Linux GUI (Graphical User Interface) as shown in Figure 2.6.

1. Leafpad full screen editor
2. LXTerminal (Lightweight X Terminal emulator) for command lines

Each of these windows can be opened from the group of accessories under the pull-down menu as show in Figure 2.7. Existing source code files can also be opened by Leafpad by double clicking them from the file explorer.

Figure 2.7: LXTerminal and Leafpad in pull-down menu

An alternate approach has been taken by many of my students where they work entirely from the command prompt. This can be done by either opening only one terminal window from the GUI or by configuring Linux to boot directly into command line mode (i.e., don't run "startx" to start the GUI). Instead of using the leafpad editor in its own window, they use an editor such as nano, vi, vim, or emacs that is opened from the command line. In this book, my edit-compile-link-execute work flow will show the nano editor being used, but please use whichever editor you prefer. Appendix E provides a few pointers on using Leafpad, nano, and vi for those who are new to editors or need a little refresher. A "word processor" program cannot be used to generate or update the assembler source code because it inserts many hidden commands for changing fonts, formatting pages, and including images that would upset the assembler.

A third approach involves remote access to the ARM computer through a router. By using a PC-based application like PuTTY, files can be edited on the PC and then either uploaded or moved into nano or vi using a copy-paste procedure (control-C on the PC and shift-insert in nano). You may obtain the IP address needed by PuTTY by entering "hostname –I" from the command prompt

2: Compile, Link, Execute

using a keyboard already attached to the ARM.

The IP address of the BeagleBone Black attached to a PC through the included USB cable is (192.168.7.2). Using the PuTTY program is a common configuration for BeagleBone Black users running in Linux command mode.

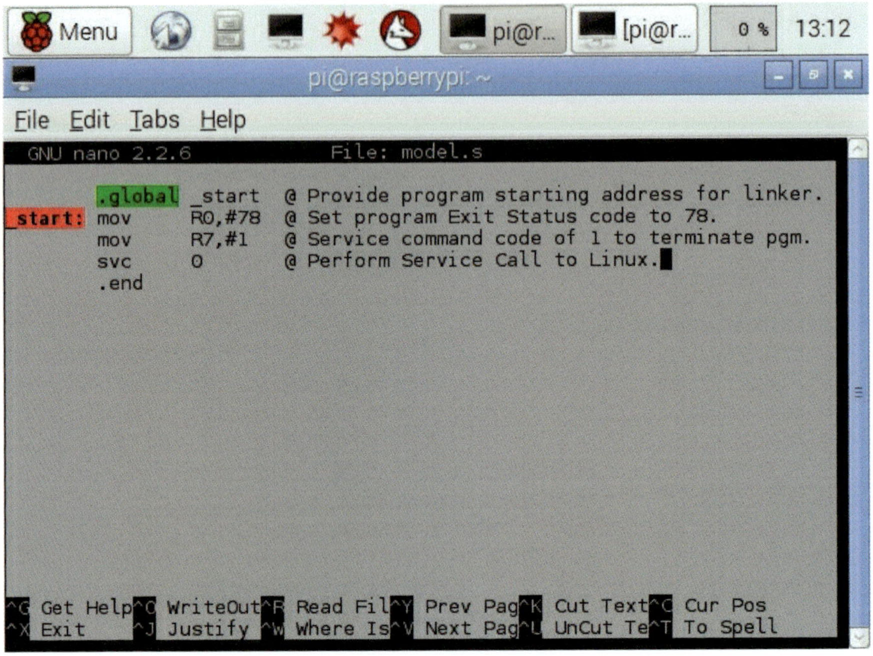

Figure 2.8: Nano editor with first program displayed.

Using the nano text editor or any other editor of your choosing, key the following very short program into a file named model.s. This is close to the shortest assembly language program you can write that does anything at all. A decimal value of 78 is loaded into register R0, and then a Linux service command is called to terminate the program.

```
        .global   _start:    @ Provide program starting address to linker
_start:   mov       R0,#78     @ Set program Exit Status code to 78 (meaning ...)
          mov       R7,#1      @ Service command code 1 terminates program.
          svc       0          @ Issue Linux command to terminate program
          .end
```

Listing 2.3: Same program, but with better comments

Assembly Language Coding in Color

Listing 2.4 provides a sequence of five GNU/Linux command lines that will be used for the next few program examples to generate and then run short computer programs written in ARM assembly language. Each command is entered in response to the command line prompt which I've shortened to simply "~$." The first three commands of Listing 2.4 generate the executable program:

1. **nano:** The first command line uses the "nano" editor program to create or update the source text file containing the assembly language code. Of course, if you are editing using leafpad in its own window, this command line is not present.
2. **as:** The GNU "as" (assembler) program reads the assembly language statements in the source text file and writes an object file containing machine code instructions.
3. **ld:** The "ld" (linker) program reads the object file, combines it with any needed utilities, and writes the executable file that is ready to run.

```
~$ nano model.s
~$ as -o model.o model.s
~$ ld -o model model.o
~$ ./model
~$ echo $?
```

Listing 2.4: Sequence of edit, compile, link, execute, display

Once you assemble this program using the "as" command, link it using the "ld" command, and execute it with the "./model" command, you can then display its output "status" value of 78 using the "echo $?" command. For a little variety, you may choose to change the 78 to some other value, but it does have an upper limit that isn't very large. Note: If you need a little background on use of nano or one of the other editors, please see Appendix E, and if the # (hash code, pound sign) character does not appear when you enter it from the keyboard, please see Appendix A.

Large Programs

In programs that are more than about 100 lines of code, you'll want to divide them into multiple source files as illustrated in Figure 2.9. Here the linker really is linking more than one object file in order to produce the complete working program. Here I've chosen three source files, but in reality hundreds of files could be involved to produce a large program. There are additional libraries and dynamic linking that can be used, but we'll leave those techniques for a different book.

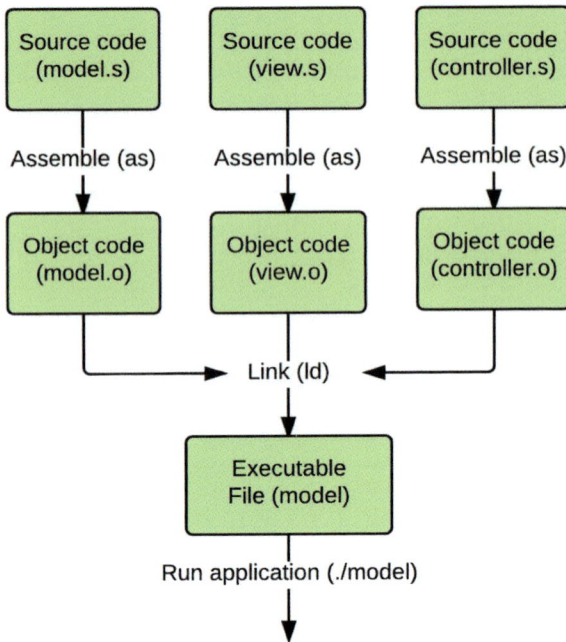

Figure 2.9: Dividing a program into modules

In figure 2.9 we see how a large program can be divided up into multiple source files and individually compiled into individual object files. These object files then have to be linked together to form a working program that can then be run.

It's good practice to enter the program yourself, but since there are hundreds of lines of program code in this book, perhaps that's too much of a good thing. Appendix A shows how all the source code for this book can be easily downloaded over the Internet using git and GitHub. Listing 12.5 shows how the above model.s program can be copied using the cp command. The ls and cat commands are not necessary, but will list the contents of the directory and the copied model.s source code, respectively.

```
~$ ls   RPi_Asm_Color
~$ cp   RPi_Asm_Color/Listing_2_3.txt   model.s
~$ cat   model.s
```

Listing 2.5: Copy existing source code used in this book

— 3 —
User Interface

Almost every CPU ever designed has an instruction that "calls" the operating system for services. We've already used the SVC (service call) instruction to terminate a program. Now we will use it to write to the display monitor and read from the keyboard. It can be used to read and write disk files and Input/Output data lines as well. Chapter 3 also introduces the use of "loops" which is a popular programming technique to perform repetitive tasks.

Linux Services

We've already been using one Linux service to quit a program. This service (having [R7]=1) is unique in that it does not return control to the instruction after the service call. The new service that we will be using ([R7]=4) will perform the task of writing to the display monitor and then returning control to the instruction following the service call.

One of the main responsibilities of an operating system, such as Linux, is to provide services for application programs. A large portion of these services involves reading and writing peripheral devices (display monitor, keyboard, mouse, network, etc.) and disk files (real spinning disks as well as solid-state memory devices). The calling program must provide Linux with the details of what is to be performed:

1. What is to be done
2. Which device is to written or read
3. Where the data (buffer) is in the program's memory
4. How much data is to be written or read

In the case of Linux, as well as most operating systems, this information is provided in the CPU's registers. For some devices such as a disk or external memory, another parameter providing the location on the disk is many times required as well.

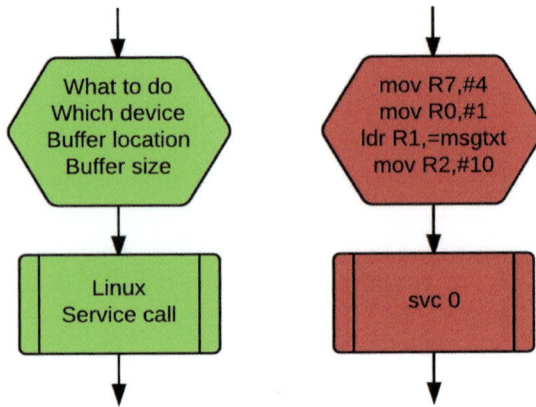

Figure 3.1: Register setup before Linux service call

In Figure 3.1, a second Linux service request is being introduced to write a string of bytes. With [R7] set to 4, the "svc 0" service call will write to the device specified by register R0. A value of [R0]=1 indicates that the string should be written to the standard output device "stdout," which is usually the computer's display monitor. The memory location of the string is loaded into R1 and its length into R2. The second "svc 0" which has [R7]=1 will terminate the program with a status code of 0 (from R0) implying a successful performance.

In Listing 3.1, I'm also introducing two more assembler directives: .data and .ascii. The .ascii directive tells the assembler to place a string of ASCII characters into memory. Special control characters can be indicated by a sequence beginning with a back slash (\n represents "line feed," hexadecimal value 0A). See Appendix D for some background on the ASCII character set if you like. The .data directive enables the assembler (with the help of the linker) to separate the areas of the computer memory dedicated to instructions from that of data values. In this example, it is not necessary, but it is setting a pattern for later programming examples.

Go ahead and run this sample program. You can use the same command sequences (Listing 2.4, as copied below), but you will not need the echo command (unless, of course, you want to see the exit status of zero). Try different text messages, but be sure to change the value in register R2 to match the length of the message.

```
1.      .global  _start                @ Program starting address for linker
2.
3. @    Program to display Hello World.
4.
5. _start:  ldr    R1,=msg             @ Load pointer to message.
6.          mov    R2,#12              @ Number of characters in message
7.          mov    R0,#1               @ Code for stdout (usually the monitor)
8.          mov    R7,#4               @ Linux service command code to write
9.          svc    0                   @ Call Linux command.
10.
11. @   Exit and return full control back to Linux.
12.
13.         mov    R7,#1               @ Command 1 terminates programs.
14.         mov    R0,#0               @ Zero "exit status" implies success.
15.         svc    0                   @ Return full control to Linux.
16.
17.         .data                      @ Begin "data" section of memory
18. msg:    .ascii    "Hello World\n"  @ ASCII string to display
19.         .end
```

Listing 3.1: Program to display "Hello World" on the monitor

In Listing 3.1, lines 6, 7, 8, 13, and 14 all use the MOV instruction to load a constant into a register. Line 5 is similar, except it uses the LDR instruction to load the address of a message in memory into a register. As stated in the previous chapter, Appendix A shows how all the source code for this book can be easily downloaded over the Internet using git and GitHub.

Notice that I've included line number for each line of the text file containing the program and data. These numbers are not actually in the text file itself, but usually provided by the editor and assembler on a temporary basis.

```
~$ nano model.s
~$ as -o model.o model.s
~$ ld -o model model.o
~$ ./model
~$ echo $?
```

Copy of Listing 2.4: Sequence of edit, compile, link, execute, display status

Read and Write

Another Linux service is one that reads from the keyboard, disk files, and I/O devices. The following register contents will be set before the SVC service call to read from the keyboard:

- [R7] = 3 (Read from device)
- [R0] = 0 (Device is "stdin" which is usually the keyboard)
- [R1] = address of memory buffer to receive input
- [R2] = maximum number of characters in buffer

Upon return from the service call, the buffer will be filled, and register R2 will contain the number of characters entered including the "line feed" character resulting from the "Enter" key. The previous program has been modified so that it now reads one line of text from the keyboard and displays it on the monitor.

```
1.          .global    _start      @ Program starting address for linker
2.
3. @        Read input line from user keyboard or redirected file.
4.
5. _start:  ldr        R1,=msg     @ Memory address to receive input
6.          mov        R0,#0       @ Stdin: Standard input (usually keyboard)
7.          mov        R7,#3       @ Linux command code to read
8.          mov        R2,#20      @ Maximum length to receive
9.          svc        0           @ Issue command to read.
10.
11. @       Echo line just input back to the user.
12.
13.         mov        R2,R0       @ Number of characters input
14.         mov        R0,#1       @ Code for stdout (usually the monitor)
15.         mov        R7,#4       @ Linux service command code to write
16.         svc        0           @ Call Linux command.
17.
18. @       Exit and return full control back to Linux.
19.
20.         mov        R7,#1       @ Command 1 terminates programs.
21.         mov        R0,#0       @ Zero "exit status" implies success.
22.         svc        0           @ Return full control to Linux.
23.         .data
24. msg:    .ds        10          @ Memory buffer for keyboard input
25.         .end
```

Listing 3.2: Read one line of text and display it.

The only new "instruction" is the .ds (define storage) assembler directive on line

24 of Listing 3.2. It reserves ten 16-bit words of memory space to hold the input data.

Program Loops

Computers are great for doing repetitive operations. A loop is a "process" that can be performed multiple times until a "decision" is made to move onto something else. Examples of processes and decisions:

- Process: Eating one mouthful of food at lunch
- Decision: Is there any more food on my plate?

- Process: Grading one student's exam
- Decision: Are there any more exams to grade?

- Process: Display one bit ("0" or "1") on the monitor
- Decision: Are there any more bits remaining to display?

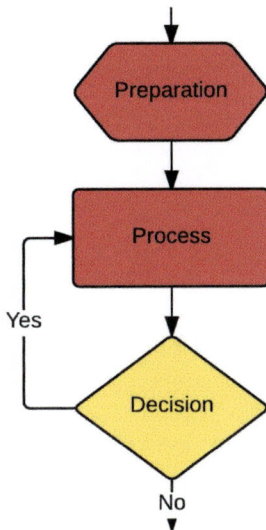

A loop consists of three parts:

1. Preparation: Set initial values for a) variables to be modified during each pass of the loop and b) variables, like counters, that will determine when to exit the loop.
2. A process to be repeated multiple times: Examples include adding numbers to a running total, searching a table for a particular value, and calling the same set of subroutines multiple times.
3. Decision when to exit the loop: Some loops such as those used in a medical device performing real-time life-support are not intended to stop. But most loops do have an exit objective such as a) all of the desired sets of numbers have been added, b) the entire table has been searched, c) the desired value has been located, etc.

Figure 3.2: Program loop

Now, the program has been modified so that it prompts the user for the input text line, still echoes the line back on the monitor, and also continues to do so until a blank line (only the "Enter" key) is pushed.

```
1.      .global    _start          @ Program starting address for linker
2.
3. @    Program to read a line from keyboard and echo it on monitor.
4.
5._start:  ldr     R1,=prompt      @ Load pointer to message.
6.         mov     R2,#27          @ Number of characters in message
7.         mov     R0,#1           @ Stdout: Standard output (usually monitor)
8.         mov     R7,#4           @ Linux command code to write
9.         svc     0               @ Call Linux command.
10.
11. @   Read input line from user keyboard or redirected file.
12.
13.        ldr     R1,=msg         @ Memory address to receive input
14.        mov     R0,#0           @ Stdin: Standard input (usually keyboard)
15.        mov     R7,#3           @ Linux command code to read
16.        mov     R2,#20          @ Maximum length to receive
17.        svc     0               @ Issue command to read.
18.
19. @   Echo line just input back to the user.
20.
21.        mov     R2,R0           @ Number of characters input
22.        mov     R0,#1           @ Code for stdout (usually the monitor)
23.        mov     R7,#4           @ Linux service command code to write
24.        svc     0               @ Call Linux command.
25.
26. @   Go get another line, but exit if only "Enter" key input.
27.
28.        cmp     R2,#1           @ Test if only the line feed character.
29.        bgt     _start          @ Loop back around to get another input.
30.        mov     R7,#1           @ Command 1 terminates programs.
31.        mov     R0,#0           @ Zero "exit status" implies success.
32.        svc     0               @ Return full control to Linux.
33.
34.        .data
35. msg:   .ds     10              @ Memory buffer for keyboard input
36. prompt:  .ascii  "Please enter text message: "
37.        .end
```

Listing 3.3: Program to echo multiple input text lines

Lines 28 and 29 test whether the loop should continue. The CMP (compare) will set bits in a status register (CPSR) based on whether [R2] is less than, greater than, or equal to the constant value of 1 (representing only the "Enter" key being pushed). The BGT (Branch if Greater Than) instruction on line 29 will take the program back to the top of the loop if the appropriate status bits in the CPSR are set.

```
~$ ./model
Please enter text message: First test line
First test line
Please enter text message: Second and last line
Second and last line
Please enter text message:

~$
```

Listing 3.4: Sample program execution: Output in red, user input in blue.

Current Program Status Register (CPSR)

Nearly every CPU ever designed has a Processor State Register which provides information regarding previous instructions that were executed (as well as other status info):

1. Was the previous result positive or negative?
2. Was the previous result zero?
3. Did the instruction end in error (like the sum of two positive numbers resulting in a negative number)?

In the ARM processor, the CPSR (Current Program Status Register) has N, Z, C, and V status flags:

N	Negative: Previous operation result was negative (i.e., bit 31 = 1)
Z	Zero: Previous operation result was zero (i.e., bits 31..0 = 0)
C	Carry: Previous operation resulted in a value that exceeded 32 bit register.
V	Overflow: Previous operation resulted in an error such as wrong positive/negative value.

Table 3.1: Status bits in the CPSR

The BGT (Branch if Greater Than) instruction is shown in the listings in two colors (red and black) because it's execution (the branch, a.k.a jump) only takes place if the proper condition exists (both N and Z status bits equal to zero). As mentioned earlier, I wanted to color the GT as yellow, but it would be too hard to see.

Nested Loops

Let's modify the program again to make it a bit more interesting. This time, we will display each character on a separate line.

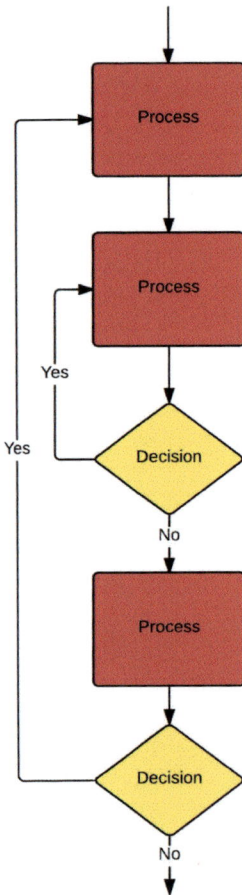

A very common programming technique is one loop nested within another. Each loop will have its own exit condition.

- The outer loop will be similar to the previous example: The user will be prompted for an input which will then be echoed back to the user on the display monitor.
- The inner loop adds the new feature in this example where each character will be on its own line. The inner loop will have register R1 initialized to point to the first character in the buffer, and also have register R4 initialized to the number of characters input.

Although nested loops are a powerful technique, it's very easy to write large nested loops with confusing code where one loop's data and counters interfere with that of the other.

Figure 3.3: Nested loops

```
 1.         .global    _start            @ Program starting address for linker
 2.
 3.@        Display prompt message.
 4.
 5._start:  ldr        R1,=prompt        @ Load pointer to message.
 6.         mov        R2,#27            @ Number of characters in message
 7.         mov        R0,#1             @ Stdout: Standard output (usually monitor)
 8.         mov        R7,#4             @ Linux command code to write
 9.         svc        0                 @ Call Linux command.
10.
11.@        Read input line from user keyboard or redirected file.
12.
13.         ldr        R1,=msg           @ Memory address to receive input
14.         mov        R0,#0             @ Stdin: Standard input (usually keyboard)
15.         mov        R7,#3             @ Linux command code to read
16.         mov        R2,#20            @ Maximum length to receive
17.         svc        0                 @ Issue command to read.
18.
19.@        Echo line just input back to the user one character at a time.
20.
21.         mov        R4,R0             @ Number of characters input in message
22.         mov        R5,R0             @ Save a copy to test for exit.
23.         mov        R0,#1             @ Code for stdout (usually the monitor)
24.         mov        R7,#4             @ Linux service command code to write
25.         mov        R2,#1             @ Display one character at a time.
26.inloop:  svc        0                 @ Display next one character of message.
27.         add        R3,R1,#1          @ Save address of next byte to be displayed.
28.         ldr        R1,=newln         @ Line feed character skips to new line.
29.         svc        0                 @ Put each input character on a separate line.
30.         mov        R1,R3             @ Restore pointer to message being displayed.
31.         subs       R4,#1             @ Decrement number of characters remaining.
32.         bgt        inloop            @ Continue loop until message complete.
33.
34.@        Go get another line, but exit if only "Enter" key was input.
35.
36.         cmp        R5,#1             @ Test if only the line feed character.
37.         bgt        _start            @ Loop back around to get another input.
38.         mov        R7,#1             @ Command 1 terminates programs.
39.         mov        R0,#0             @ Zero "exit status" implies success.
40.         svc        0                 @ Return full control to Linux.
41.
42.         .data
43.msg:     .ds        10                @ Memory buffer for keyboard input
44.prompt:  .ascii     "Please enter text message: "
45.newln:   .ascii     "\n"              @ Line feed character code
46.         .end
```

Listing 3.5: Nested loop that echoes input text lines one character at a time

The inner loop is on lines 26 through 32 of Listing 3.5. The following registers control which character is displayed and when the loop should be exited:

- R3 and R1 point to the next character to display. The ADD instruction on line 27 is [R3] = [R1] + 1.

- R4 contains the number of characters remaining to display.

Lines 28 and 29 test whether the loop should continue. The CMP (compare) will set status bits.

```
~$ ./model
Please enter text message: First line
F
i
r
s
t

l
i
n
e

Please enter text message: Last
L
a
s
t

Please enter text message:

~$
```

Listing 3.6: Echo each character on its own line.

— 4 —
Subroutines & Macros

One of the principal hallmarks of the industrial revolution was the use of interchangeable parts in the manufacturing process. In a similar manner, subroutines, macros, and operating system services are building blocks for developing large sophisticated software applications. These three building blocks are predefined program segments that can be used over and over again by calling them from the application program.

- Service: A section of operating system code that is "jumped to" or "branched to" to perform a common task for all user programs.
- Subroutine: A section of user-written code that is "jumped to" or "branched to" to perform a common task within a user program.
- Macro: A section of user-written code that is "copied and pasted" into multiple locations within the program source code.

As already seen with Linux services, the exact actions performed by these building blocks can be modified slightly based on a set of input parameters referred to as "arguments."

Subroutines

A subroutine is a section of code that is "called" to perform a specific job. Depending upon the programming language and application, subroutines are also known as functions, modules, procedures, and methods. Examples of jobs a subroutine can perform:

- Display a number to the user
- Get keyboard input from the user
- Get input from a specific device such as a temperature sensor
- Change the speed of a motor
- Perform a particular type of analysis such as a least-squares fit of data

The advantages of using subroutines are many:

- Subroutines help organize the construction of the program.
- The code only takes up memory space once.
- It's less work to modify or correct one area of common code rather than many copies of almost identical code.

- "Information hiding" occurs because one part of the program is unable to directly access data in another part of the program and accidentally change it.
- Division of programming assignments among different programmers is easier.

The disadvantages of subroutines are few.

- There is a slight performance degradation compared to "in-line code" due to the overhead of the call and return.
- It can lead to too much of a good thing: Too many tiny subroutines can lead to confusion.

The program from Chapter 3 will now be modified by adding a very simple subroutine, v_asc1, which will display one ASCII character on the display monitor. In the ARM architecture, the BL (branch and link) instruction will be used to call subroutine v_asc1 in a manner similar to how the SVC (service call) instruction calls operating system services. After performing their assigned tasks, subroutines and services return program control to the instruction following the point from which they were called. In the ARM architecture, the BX (branch exchange) instruction is usually the best way to return from a subroutine.

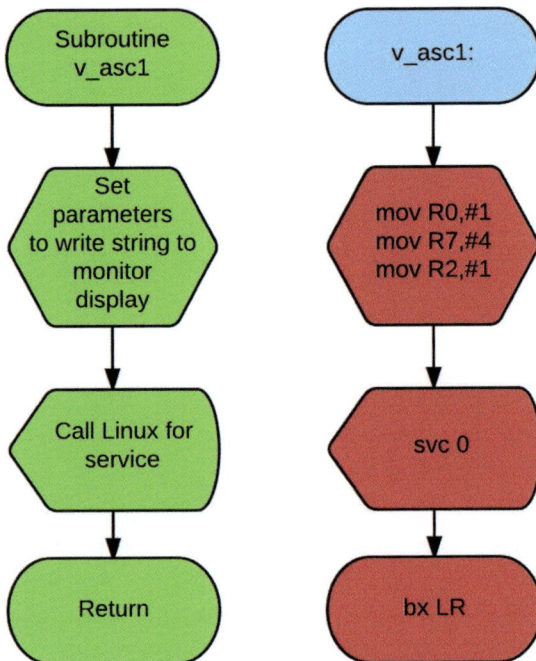

Figure 4.1: Subroutine v_asc1 displays one character

Assembly Language Coding in Color

The first 45 lines of the program in Listing 4.1 are the same as those in Listing 3.5 except for lines 26 and 29 where the SVC service call has been replaced by a BL instruction to call subroutine v_asc1.

```
1.          .global    _start           @ Program starting address for linker
2.
3. @        Display prompt message.
4.
5. _start:  ldr        R1,=prompt       @ Load pointer to message.
6.          mov        R2,#27           @ Number of characters in message
7.          mov        R0,#1            @ Stdout: Standard output (usually monitor)
8.          mov        R7,#4            @ Linux command code to write
9.          svc        0                @ Call Linux command.
10.
11. @       Read input line from user keyboard or redirected file.
12.
13.         ldr        R1,=msg          @ Memory address to receive input
14.         mov        R0,#0            @ Stdin: Standard input (usually keyboard)
15.         mov        R7,#3            @ Linux command code to read
16.         mov        R2,#20           @ Maximum length to receive
17.         svc        0                @ Issue command to read.
18.
19. @       Echo line just input back to the user one character at a time.
20.
21.         mov        R4,R0            @ Number of characters input in message
22.         mov        R5,R0            @ Save a copy to test for exit.
23.         mov        R0,#1            @ Code for stdout (usually the monitor)
24.         mov        R7,#4            @ Linux service command code to write
25.         mov        R2,#1            @ Display one character at a time.
26. inloop: bl         v_asc1           @ Display next one character of message.
27.         add        R3,R1,#1         @ Save address of next byte to be displayed.
28.         ldr        R1,=newln        @ Line feed character skips to new line.
29.         bl         v_asc1           @ Put each input character on a separate line.
30.         mov        R1,R3            @ Restore pointer to message being displayed.
31.         subs       R4,#1            @ Decrement number of characters remaining.
32.         bgt        inloop           @ Continue loop until message complete.
33.
34. @       Go get another line, but exit if only "Enter" key was input.
35.
36.         cmp        R5,#1            @ Test if only the line feed character.
37.         bgt        _start           @ Loop back around to get another input.
38.         mov        R7,#1            @ Command 1 terminates programs.
39.         mov        R0,#0            @ Set exit code to zero.
40.         svc        0                @ Return full control to Linux.
41.
42.         .data
43. msg:    .ds        10               @ Memory buffer for keyboard input
44. prompt: .ascii     "Please enter text message: "
```

45. newln:	.ascii	"\n"	@ Line feed character code
46.	.text		
47.			
48. @		Subroutine v_asc1 will display one character from memory buffer.	
49. @		R1: Points to character in memory	
50. @		LR: Contains the return address	
51. @		SP: Stack pointer	
52. @		All register contents will be preserved.	
53.			
54. v_asc1:	push	{R0,R2,R7}	@ Save contents of registers to be used.
55.	mov	R0,#1	@ Code for stdout (usually the monitor)
56.	mov	R7,#4	@ Linux service command code to write
57.	mov	R2,#1	@ Display one character at a time.
58.	svc	0	@ Display next one character of message.
59.	pop	{R0,R2,R7}	@ Restore saved register contents.
60.	bx	LR	@ Return to the calling program.
61.	.end		

Listing 4.1: Model program with subroutine v_asc1

Four additional instructions are introduced in Listing 4.1:

- Branch and link (BL): Calls a subroutine by saving the address of the instruction following the BL in the link register (LR) and then branching (also known as jumping in many CPU architectures) to a another location in the program.
- Branch exchange (BX): Returns from a subroutine by branching to the program location specified in a register.
- Push: Save register contents in a special reserved memory area known as the "stack."
- Pop: Reload registers from data previously saved on the stack.

There is also an additional assembler directive introduced on line 46. The .text directive reverses the .data directive, and tells the assembler it should include the code following it in the same area of memory as the previous instruction group.

Subroutine v_asc1 is so simple, you might ask, "Why bother at all, just use the Linux SVC directly and reduce the additional overhead of a subroutine essentially calling the same type of subroutine." In a very small program with only a few calls to display, I would agree. However, for larger programs, a dedicated display subroutine provides a lot of flexibility from the maintenance perspective. Just for example, let's say we have developed a program with thousands of calls to display, and now the "marketplace" requires that we send our display messages to a different device (one that the simple Linux call cannot perform). Wouldn't it be more convenient to accommodate that change in one place in the subroutine's code rather than hunt it down in the large program and try to successfully change it thousands of times?

As Listing 4.1 illustrates, the operation of every subroutine should be internally documented in comments:

1. Name of the subroutine and what it does
2. Resources it needs (R1 points to the string to be displayed).
3. How the subroutine is going to return to the program that called it (LR register contains the return address)
4. What is in the registers when the subroutine is complete and returns to the calling program

Efficiency vs. Maintenance

If you examine the code in Listing 4.1, you notice that registers R0, R2, and R7 are set up for the Linux SVC to display one character on the monitor. They are loaded with the same values on lines 55 through 57 in subroutine v_asc1 as they were in the main program on lines 23 through 25. Although the program output is identical whether a register is loaded once or even a hundred times with the same value, it is somewhat confusing and slightly inefficient.

From an efficiency perspective, it is better to load the registers in the main program once rather than each time the subroutine is called. However, from a program maintenance standpoint, it is better to load the registers close to where they will be used, i.e., in the subroutine. Keeping the arguments for a subroutine as simple as possible enables the program to be more easily modified in the future. In the next modification to the program appearing in Listing 4.2, the registers will only be initialized in the subroutine.

Registers R13, R14, R15

The ARM processor has 16 general purpose registers, R0 through R15, each having 32-bits. By "general purpose," we mean the registers can be used both in arithmetic calculations as well as addressing memory. Three of these registers also have a special purpose as described below:

- R13, also known as SP (Stack Pointer)
- R14, also known as LR (Link Register)
- R15, also known as PC (Program Counter)

Program Counter (PC)

The PC register contains the memory address of the next instruction to be executed. On approximately one half of all CPUs, it is referred to as the IP (Instruction Pointer) instead of the PC, but they perform the same function. For every instruction except branch instructions, the address of the next instruction will be the one immediately following it in memory. During the execution of an instruction, the CPU automatically increments the PC to the address of the instruction immediately following it in memory. This is an increment by four because all ARM-format instructions are four bytes long.

In the ARM, the PC can also be changed in other ways because the PC is also register R15, which is a general purpose register. So you could skip over a few instructions with "ADD R15,#8" or even "ADD PC,#8." You could return from a subroutine with a "MOV R15,R14," instead of a "BX LR" instruction, but I generally don't recommend any of these. If you do something cute, and it saves a worthwhile amount of execution time, please document it in your code. Remember: The object of writing good code does not include trying to confuse and aggravate the person maintaining the code a few years later.

Link Register (LR)

In the ARM architecture, a subroutine is typically called using the branch and link (BL) instruction which loads the address of the instruction following the BL instruction into the LR link register. The idea is to provide the subroutine with a return address. Over the decades, this has been done in many different CPU architectures with instructions named BALR (Branch and Link Register), LMJ (Load Modifier and Jump), SLJ (Store Location and Jump), RJ (Return Jump), and of course CALL (not an acronym, just plain "call"). BALR and LMJ provided the return address in a register, while SLJ and RJ put it into the first word of the subroutine's memory, and CALL saved the return address onto the "stack."

A subroutine must be careful not to accidentally lose its return address. If one subroutine calls another, the contents of the LR must be saved beforehand otherwise the second BL will overwrite it. Also, the LR is a second name for register R14 which can be used as a general purpose accumulator.

Stack Pointer (SP) Register

The SP register points to the "top" of the stack, an area of memory where temporary data may be stored. Although the concept of a memory stack has been used from the early days, instructions that explicitly use one didn't become popular until appearing on many computers like the DEC PDP 11 in the mid-1970s. Characteristics of a stack:

- A common metaphor of stack operation is the placing and getting of cafeteria trays and plates. You place new trays on top and also remove trays from the top. Who would try to take the tray on the very bottom or from the middle of a stack?
- Data is stored onto and retrieved from the stack in a LIFO (Last In, First Out) manner.
- Stack usage is very easy: You "push" new data onto the stack and "pop" the most recent data from the top of the stack. The pushing and popping user does not have to know the details of where in memory the stack is actually located and exactly how it works.
- The area of memory allocated to the stack and the SP pointer contents are set up by Linux when it starts each program.
- In the ARM, the SP is also register R13, which is a general purpose accumulator.
- The stack is a great way to save or allocate memory for temporary variables in a subroutine.
- A stack enables the construction of recursive subroutines that call themselves.
- It is possible to "blow" the stack by pushing more data onto it than it was reserved to handle.

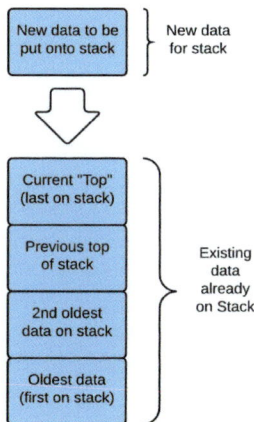

Figure 4.2: Stack "concept"

What do we mean by "pushing data on top of the stack" or "popping data from the top of the stack"?

Figure 4.2 illustrates pushing a value onto a stack that already contains four values. The size of each value can vary among applications and CPU architectures. The PUSH instruction not only stores data from one or more registers into the stack area of memory, but also updates the SP register. The POP instruction does the reverse: It loads one or more registers from data in memory and also updates the SP.

Macros

Almost all assemblers for all CPU designs have some form of "macro" capability, and the GNU "as" assembler is no exception. Macros provide a means for generating custom data formats and custom sequences of instructions. They not only provide for quicker initial program development, but also provide better documentation and maintenance.

As shown in Listing 4.2, a macro begins with the .macro statement and ends with .endm. Macro processors for other ARM assemblers may begin with macro and end with mend, so macro syntax is not portable among all assemblers, even for the same CPU architecture.

```
 1.      .global    _start           @ Program starting address for linker
 2.
 3. @         Macro "disp sub,tail" calls a subroutine, then displays a character.
 4. @                   sub:   Subroutine to be called
 5. @                   tail:  Separation character to be output
 6.
 7.      .macro     disp   sub, tail
 8.      bl         \sub             @ Call desired subroutine.
 9.      push       {R1}             @ Save value that is in R1.
10.      ldr        R1,=\tail        @ Separation character.
11.      bl         v_asc1           @ Display single character.
12.      pop        {R1}             @ Restore original value in R1.
13.      .endm
14.
15. @         Display prompt message.
16.
17. _start: ldr       R1,=prompt       @ Load pointer to message.
18.      mov        R2,#27           @ Number of characters in message
19.      mov        R0,#1            @ Stdout: Standard output (usually monitor)
20.      mov        R7,#4            @ Linux command code to write
21.      svc        0                @ Call Linux command.
22.
23. @         Read input line from user keyboard or redirected file.
24.
25.      ldr        R1,=msg          @ Memory address to receive input
26.      mov        R0,#0            @ Stdin: Standard input (usually keyboard)
27.      mov        R7,#3            @ Linux command code to read
28.      mov        R2,#20           @ Maximum length to receive
29.      svc        0                @ Issue command to read.
30.
31. @         Echo line just input back to the user one character at a time.
32.
33.      mov        R5,R0            @ Save a copy to test for exit.
34. inloop: disp     v_asc1,newln     @ Display next character and line feed.
```

35.	add	R1,#1	@ Set address to next character in buffer.
36.	subs	R0,#1	@ Decrement number of characters remaining.
37.	bgt	inloop	@ Continue loop until message complete.
38.			
39. @		Go get another line, but exit if only "Enter" key was input.	
40.			
41.	cmp	R5,#1	@ Test if only the line feed character.
42.	bgt	_start	@ Loop back around to get another input.
43.	mov	R7,#1	@ Command 1 terminates programs.
44.	mov	R0,#0	@ Set exit code to zero.
45.	svc	0	@ Return full control to Linux.
46.			
47.	.data		
48. msg:	.ds	10	@ Memory buffer for keyboard input
49. prompt:	.ascii	"Please enter text message: "	
50. newln:	.ascii	"\n"	@ Line feed character code
51.	.end		

Listing 4.2: Macro disp simplifies calling two subroutines.

Macros typically generate more than one line of assembler code for each macro call line. Macro processing is performed during a first pass through the assembler source file that expands macro statements before the assembler converts them to machine code. You can think of a macro as a subroutine that is called at assembly time. Instead of performing a calculation using the contents of the registers, it generates lines of assembly language code that will be included in the program. Arguments appear after the macro name and are used to provide differences in the assembly language code that is generated.

As shown on line 7, the "disp" macro is called with two arguments: "sub" and "tail." Wherever "sub" appears in the text of the macro following a back slash, the value from the macro call line will be substituted. Likewise, wherever "\tail" appears in the text of the macro, the value from the macro call line will be substituted.

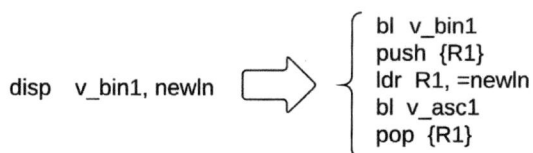

disp v_bin1, newln ⟹
```
bl  v_bin1
push {R1}
ldr R1, =newln
bl  v_asc1
pop {R1}
```

Figure 4.3: Macro expansion generates assembly language instructions.

Figure 4.3 shows an example of the macro expansion: Five lines of assembler source code are generated by one "disp" macro call. It produces two subroutine calls: The first is specified in the first argument, while the second is always v_asc1. Notice that this macro will preserve the contents of register R1 on the stack using PUSH and POP.

You have probably noticed that I did not include subroutine v_asc1 in the model.s source file provided in Listing 4.2. I have moved it to a separate file all by itself as seen in Listing 4.3

1. @		Subroutine v_asc1 will display one character from memory buffer.	
2. @		R1: Points to character in memory	
3. @		LR: Contains the return address	
4. @		SP: Stack pointer	
5. @		All register contents will be preserved.	
6.			
7.	.global	v_asc1	@ Externalize the subroutine entry point.
8.			
9. v_asc1:	push	{R0,R2,R7}	@ Save contents of register to be used.
10.	mov	R0,#1	@ Code for stdout (usually the monitor)
11.	mov	R7,#4	@ Linux service command code to write
12.	mov	R2,#1	@ Display one character at a time.
13.	svc	0	@ Display next one character of message.
14.	pop	{R0,R2,R7}	@ Restore saved register contents.
15.	bx	LR	@ Return to the calling program.
16.	.end		

Listing 4.3: Subroutine v_asc1 in file v_asc1.s

Since we have broken the source code into two files instead of one, we now have a new work flow provided in Listing 4.4. Both source files must be edited and compiled, and now the linker is really doing its job of "linking." The linker needs the .global assembler directive in file v_asc1.s to connect its entry point to its calling point in the main program in the model.s file.

The "ld" command line now contains the name of the executable file followed by each of the object files to link, all separated by one or more blanks. The linker step will be needed for each program change, but only the source code file that is changed will need to be recompiled (i.e., reassembled). We will still be naming the executable file "model" even though it's built from both the model.o and v_ascz.o object files.

```
~$ nano model.s
~$ as -o model.o model.s
~$ nano v_asc1.s
~$ as -o v_asc1.o v_asc1.s
~$ ld -o model model.o v_asc1.o
~$ ./model
Please enter text message:
```

Listing 4.4: Sequence of edit, compile, link, and execute

— 5 —
Binary & Hexadecimal

What's wrong with decimal? Babbage's Analytical Engine computer design was decimal. Have we digressed in the past 200 years? Actually, there have been many decimal-based computers, but why are almost all of today's computers based on binary? The simple answer is that the logical building blocks (i.e., electronics in today's systems) are simpler and more efficient in binary than they are in decimal. If you are new to binary numbers, please see Appendix B or search the Internet to get some background.

A decimal number is really a short notation for a polynomial of powers of 10. For example: 137 is $1 \times 10^2 + 3 \times 10^1 + 7 \times 10^0$. Likewise, a binary number is really a short notation for a polynomial of powers of 2. For example: 110101 is $1 \times 2^5 + 1 \times 2^4 + 0 \times 2^3 + 1 \times 2^2 + 0 \times 2^1 + 1 \times 2^0$. By the way, this polynomial structure is the main reason we count bits from right to left starting with zero.

Binary computers store and manipulate bits (binary digits). Numbers are represented by "groups of bits" as either integers or real numbers. That's fine for science and engineering applications, but what's stored in "groups of bits" for business applications, such as correspondence, reports, and mailing lists? How is this text data consisting of letters, digits, and punctuation represented by "groups of bits"? A character code is a set that assigns each text character to a unique number. In Chapter 5, the model program from previous chapters will be modified to display the ASCII character code in binary and hexadecimal for each character that is entered from the keyboard.

A new subroutine (v_bin1) will be coded to display a character in memory as a series of 8 binary digits (bits). The specifications for using v_bin1 are the following:

1. The subroutine name is v_bin1 and it's purpose is to display an 8-bit value.
2. It's input argument (i.e., resources it needs) is a character in memory pointed to by register R1.
3. The return from subroutine v_bin1 is to the address in the LR (Link Register).
4. The contents of some registers will be altered by subroutine v_bin1, so it will save their original values on the stack and restore them just before returning to the calling program.

Loop Through 8 Binary Digits (Bits)

How does subroutine v_bin work? We build a loop which counts down from 7 (the position of the leftmost bit) to 0 (the position of the rightmost bit). Register R6 not only counts down from 7 to 0, but also indicates which bit is examined on each pass through the loop.

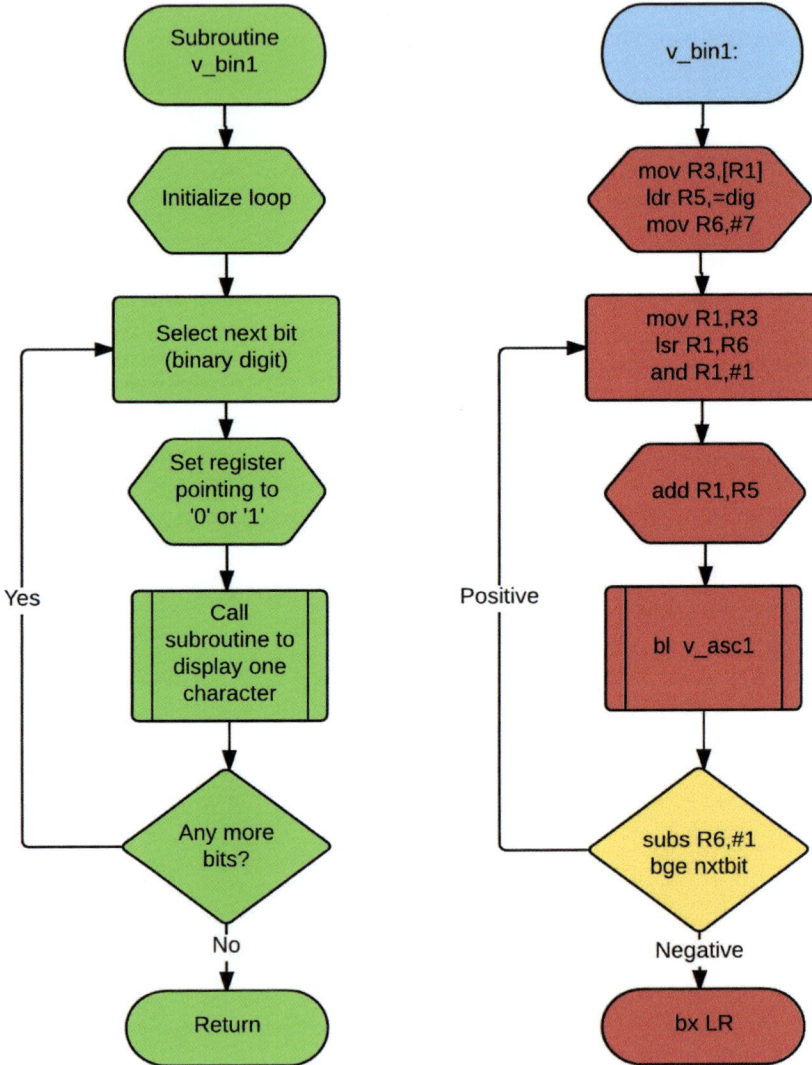

Figure 5.1: Subroutine v_bin1 design

```
 1. @       Subroutine v_bin1 displays one byte from memory in binary.
 2. @               R1: Points to byte in memory
 3. @               LR: Contains the return address
 4. @               All register contents will be preserved.
 5.
 6.      .global   v_bin1          @ Externalize the entry address.
 7.
 8. v_bin1:  push    {R0–R6,LR}    @ Save registers R0 through R6, LR.
 9.          ldrb    R3,[R1]       @ Load byte to be displayed.
10.          ldr     R5,=dig       @ Pointer to "01" ASCII string
11.          mov     R6,#7         @ Bit 7 will be output first.
12.
13. @       Loop through each bit outputing it to the standard output display.
14.
15. nxtbit:  mov     R1,R3         @ Copy byte to be displayed to R1.
16.          lsr     R1,R6         @ Shift current bit to bit 0.
17.          and     R1,#1         @ Mask off all bits except bit 0.
18.          add     R1,R5         @ Set R1 pointing to "0" or "1"
19.          bl      v_asc1        @ Display either "0" or "1".
20.          subs    R6,#1         @ Decrement number of bits to display
21.          bge     nxtbit        @ Go display next bit until all 8 displayed
22.
23.          pop     {R0–R6,LR}    @ Restore saved register contents
24.          bx      LR            @ Return to the calling program
25.
26. dig:     .ascii  "01"          @ ASCII string of binary digits 0 and 1
27.          .end
```

Listing 5.1: Subroutine to output binary number in ASCII

Each pass through the loop selects a particular bit by shifting, masking, and then pointing to either "0" or "1" in memory. As shown in Listing 5.1, the loop is between lines 15 and 21.

- Line 16: LSR - Logical Shift Right to move data bit into position
- Line 17: AND - Logical AND to remove unwanted bits
- Line 18: ADD - Generate pointer to "0" or "1"

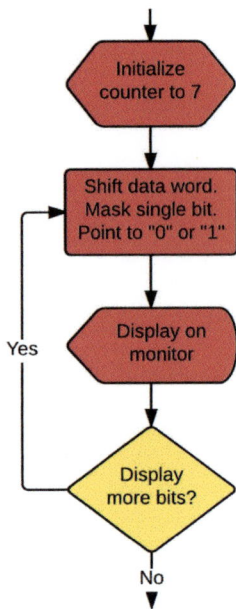

Figure 5.2: Program loop to display 8 bits

Instructions in the loop select a particular bit, convert it to ASCII, and call subroutine v_asc1 to output the one character to the monitor screen.

1. Preparation: Set initial value of "count down" register R6 to 7. R6 also points to the first bit in the data (loaded into register R3).
2. A process to be repeated multiple times: Select the next bit, indicated by value in R6, and display it as either an ASCII "0" or "1" on the monitor.
3. Decision when to exit the loop: Register R6 is decremented by one on each pass through the loop which allows it to point to all bit positions 7 through 0. When R6 is decremented from 0 to -1, then an exit from the loop is taken because all 8 bit positions have been displayed.

The SUBS (line 20) is identical to the SUB instruction, except it also sets status flags as a result of the subtraction. If R6 is decremented from 0 to -1, then the "N" flag will be set indicating a negative number. The BGE instruction (branch if greater or equal) then uses this "N" flag to know whether to branch back to continue the loop ("N" is clear implying greater or equal to zero) or not branch, thereby falling out of the loop.

Bit Shift Operations

Almost all CPU architectures include several instructions for shifting bits within a register. Most CPU architectures support three types of shifts:

- Logical: Bits shifted out from either end of the register are discarded and new zero bits fill in on the opposite side.
- Circular (also referred to as rotate): Bits shifted out one end of the register come back in on the other side.
- Arithmetic: This is similar to a logical right shift except arithmetic shift brings in copies of the sign bit instead of zero.

Assembly Language Coding in Color

Logical shifts have many applications. One common application is converting between serial and parallel, and a second is for multiplying an integer by a power of two. For example, a one bit shift to the left is multiplying by two, while a two bit shift is multiplying by four. Some computers shift only one bit at a time. In the ARM, multiple bit shifts can be indicated either from the contents of a register or an immediate value in the instruction.

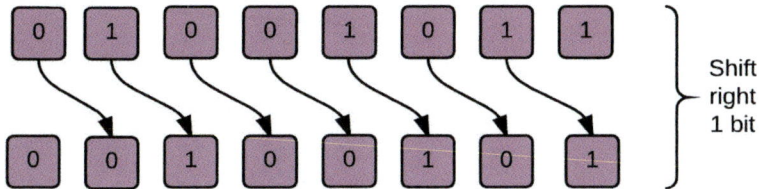

Figure 5.3: Logical right shift moves out bit on right and brings in zero on left.

A shift to the right is like dividing by a power of two, but be aware of two basic problems. Division can have a remainder which will get truncated, not rounded. Secondly, there are two problems with negative integers. A logical right shift will bring in a zero in bit 31, thereby converting a negative number to an inappropriate positive number. The arithmetic shift will solve the negative problem, but a rounding error is still present in the ARM architecture, so be careful using shifts to divide negative numbers. Please see Appendix B if you need an explanation why the high-order bit (bit 31) is a "1" for negative numbers

A circular shift, also referred to as a rotate, allows the bits to be shifted without losing anything out one end or the other. The ARM only provides a rotate to the right, but a rotate to the left can be done by a right rotate. For example, a left rotate of 5 bit positions is identical to rotating right 27 bit positions (32 minus 5). There is also an extended right rotate of one bit that copies bit 0 into a status bit known as "carry."

Logical Operations

The ARM processor provides the Boolean AND, inclusive OR, and exclusive OR logical operations. The AND will be used here in Chapter 5, while examples using the two OR operations will appear in Chapter 7.

AND

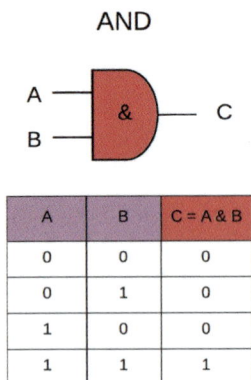

A	B	C = A & B
0	0	0
0	1	0
1	0	0
1	1	1

Figure 5.4: AND operation truth table

The truth table in Figure 5.4 gives the four possible outputs for an AND gate having two inputs.

1. If inputs A and B are both 0, the output will be 0.
2. If A is 0 and B is 1, the output will be 0.
3. If A is 1 and B is 0, the output will be 0.
4. Only if both A and B are 1 will the output be 1.

In the loop in subroutine v_dig1, the AND instruction will remove all data bits except for the bit position currently being examined.

The logical instructions in almost all CPUs are "bitwise" logical operations:

- In the ARM, thirty-two logical operations are performed in parallel. Figure 5.5 only shows a portion of the 32 pairs of corresponding bits being ANDed together.
- Figure 5.5 illustrates the AND instruction. The inclusive OR (ORR) and exclusive OR (EOR) are also bitwise instructions using 32 pairs of bits, and they will be demonstrated in Chapter 7.

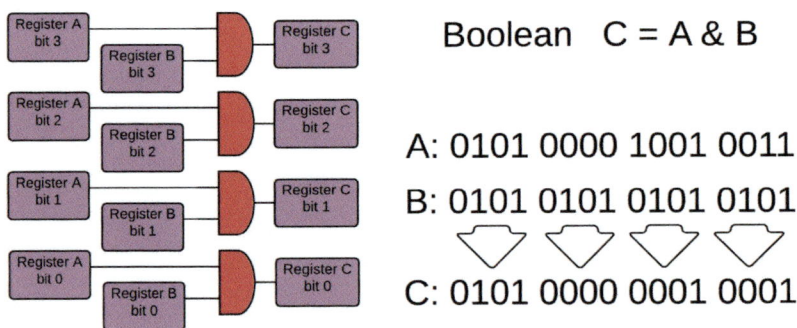

Boolean C = A & B

A: 0101 0000 1001 0011
B: 0101 0101 0101 0101
▽   ▽   ▽   ▽
C: 0101 0000 0001 0001

Figure 5.5: Examples of "bitwise" AND of two values

Figure 5.6 shows the combination of the LSR and AND instructions to select the bit from position 3 and put it into bit position 0 all by itself. In the next chapter, we will see how this can even be done with just one instruction.

Assembly Language Coding in Color

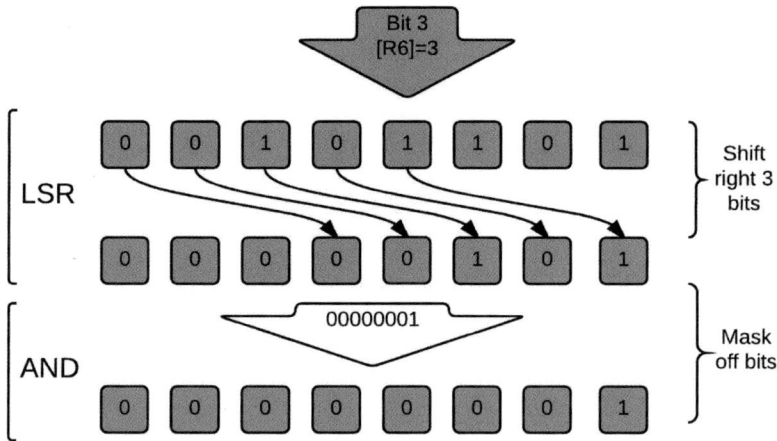

Figure 5.6: Isolate desired bit using LSR and AND instructions.

The model "main" program will now be slightly modified (indicated by the lines of text in color) to display each character in both ASCII and binary.

1.	.global	_start	@ Program starting address for linker
2.			
3. @	Macro "disp sub,tail" calls a subroutine, then displays a character.		
4. @		sub: Subroutine to be called	
5. @		tail: Separation character to be output	
6.			
7.	.macro	disp	sub,tail
8.	bl	\sub	@ Call desired subroutine.
9.	push	{R1}	@ Save value that is in R1.
10.	ldr	R1,=\tail	@ Separation character.
11.	bl	v_asc1	@ Display single character.
12.	pop	{R1}	@ Restore original value in R1.
13.	.endm		
14.			
15. @	Display prompt message.		
16.			
17. _start:	ldr	R1,=prompt	@ Load pointer to message.

18.	mov	R2,#27	@ Number of characters in message
19.	mov	R0,#1	@ Stdout: Standard output (usually monitor)
20.	mov	R7,#4	@ Linux command code to write
21.	svc	0	@ Call Linux command.
22.			
23. @		Read input line from user keyboard or redirected file.	
24.			
25.	ldr	R1,=msg	@ Memory address to receive input
26.	mov	R0,#0	@ Stdin: Standard input (usually keyboard)
27.	mov	R7,#3	@ Linux command code to read
28.	mov	R2,#20	@ Maximum length to receive
29.	svc	0	@ Issue command to read.
30.			
31. @		Echo line just input back to the user one character at a time.	
32.			
33.	mov	R5,R0	@ Save a copy to test for exit.
34. inloop:	disp	v_bin1,tab	@ Display binary of character, then tab.
35.	disp	v_asc1,newln	@ Display ASCII for character, then line feed.
36.	add	R1,#1	@ Set address to next character in buffer.
37.	subs	R0,#1	@ Decrement number of characters remaining.
38.	bgt	inloop	@ Continue loop until message complete.
39.			
40. @		Go get another line, but exit if only "Enter" key was input.	
41.			
42.	cmp	R5,#1	@ Test if only the line feed character.
43.	bgt	_start	@ Loop back around to get another input.
44.	mov	R7,#1	@ Command 1 terminates programs.
45.	mov	R0,#0	@ Set exit code to zero.
46.	svc	0	@ Return full control to Linux.
47.			
48.	.data		
49. msg:	.ds	10	@ Memory buffer for keyboard input
50. prompt:	.ascii	"Please enter text message: "	
51. newln:	.ascii	"\n"	@ Line feed character code
52. tab:	.ascii	"\t"	@ Horizontal tab character code
53.	.end		

Listing 5.2: Program to display in both binary and ASCII

The disp macro will now be more useful because it is called twice, once to display a byte in binary and once to display it in ASCII. The separator character after the binary display will be a tab, and a line feed (a.k.a., new line) character forces a new line after the ASCII character.

Listing 5.3 shows both the model.s and v_bin1.s source files being edited and compiled. The v_asc1 subroutine has not been changed so its object module v_asc1.o does not need to be updated. The linker command now includes four files: the executable "model" file as well as the three object files.

```
~$ nano model.s
~$ as -o model.o model.s
~$ nano v_bin1.s
~$ as -o v_bin1.o v_bin1.s
~$ ld -o model model.o v_asc1.o v_bin1.o
~$ ./model
Please enter text message: Hi there
01001000         H
01101001         i
00100000
01110100         t
01101000         h
01100101         e
01110010         r
01100101         e
00100001         !
00001010

Please enter text message:

~$
```

Listing 5.3: Model program with both binary and ASCII of each character,

Hexadecimal Display

Why use hexadecimal (base 16)? The simple answer is hexadecimal is compact, and it is very easy for us humans to convert between binary and hexadecimal.

Binary numbers are awkward for us due to the large number of columns required. Who would prefer replacing the decimal representation of 7094, 1620, 1108, 6600, 3033, and 7800 with their binary equivalents 1101110110110, 11001010100, 10001010100, 1100111001000, 101111011001, and 1111001111000? Conversion between binary and decimal is difficult to do "in our heads." The difficulty stems from the fact that 10 is not an integer power of two, but base 16 is 2^4 thereby making it easy to convert every 4-bit pattern to a hexadecimal digit. Please see Appendix C for more information on hexadecimal.

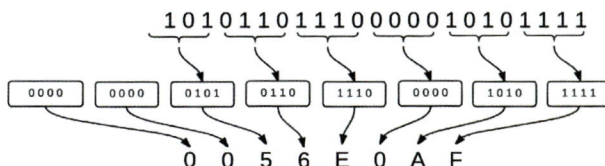

Figure 5.7: Binary reduced to hexadecimal

Subroutine v_hex1 is almost identical to subroutine v_bin1 except four bits are shifted and masked instead of just one.

1. @		Subroutine v_hex1 displays one byte in hexadecimal.	
2. @		R1: Points to byte in memory	
3. @		LR: Contains the return address	
4. @		All register contents will be preserved.	
5.			
6.	.global	v_hex1	@ Externalize the entry address.
7.			
8. v_hex1:	push	{R0−R6,LR}	@ Save registers R0 through R6, LR.
9.	ldrb	R3,[R1]	@ Load byte to be displayed.
10.	ldr	R5,=dig	@ Pointer to "0123456789ABCDEF"
11.	mov	R6,#4	@ Bit 4 will be output first.
12.			
13. @		Loop through groups of 4-bit nibbles and output each to stdout.	
14.			
15. nxthex:	mov	R1,R3	@ Copy byte to be displayed to R1.
16.	lsr	R1,R6	@ Select next hex digit (0 .. F).
17.	and	R1,#0b1111	@ Mask off all bits except lower 4.
18.	add	R1,R5	@ Set R1 pointing to "0", "1", ... or "F"
19.	bl	v_asc1	@ Display 1 hexadecimal digit "0", ...
20.	subs	R6,#4	@ Decrement number of bits to display
21.	bge	nxthex	@ Go display next nibble
22.			
23.	pop	{R0−R6,LR}	@ Restore saved register contents
24.	bx	LR	@ Return to the calling program
25.			
26. dig:	.ascii	"0123456789"	@ ASCII string of digits 0 through 9
27.	.ascii	"ABCDEF"	@ ASCII string of digits A through F
28.	.end		

Listing 5.4: Subroutine to output hexadecimal number in ASCII

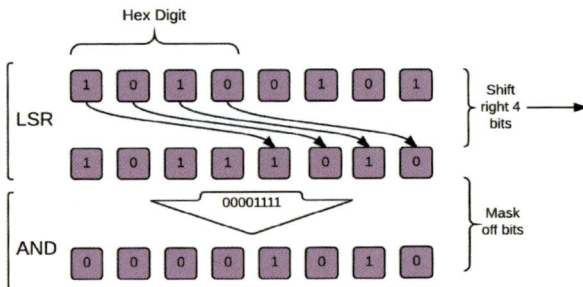

Figure 5.8: Isolate desired hex digit using LSR and AND instructions.

Assembly Language Coding in Color

The only modification made to the model "main" program shown in L
is to include a hexadecimal display. The disp macro is now even m
because it is called three times: binary, hexadecimal, and ASCII.

1.	.global	_start	@ Program starting address for linker
2.			
3. @		Macro "disp sub,tail" calls a subroutine, then displays a character.	
4. @		sub:	Subroutine to be called
5. @		tail:	Sepation character to be output
6.			
7.	.macro	disp	sub,tail
8.	bl	\sub	@ Call desired subroutine.
9.	push	{R1}	@ Save value that is in R1.
10.	ldr	R1,=\tail	@ Separation character.
11.	bl	v_ascl	@ Display single character.
12.	pop	{R1}	@ Restore original value in R1.
13.	.endm		
14.			
15. @		Display prompt message.	
16.			
17. _start:	ldr	R1,=prompt	@ Load pointer to message.
18.	mov	R2,#27	@ Number of characters in message
19.	mov	R0,#1	@ Stdout: Standard output (usually monitor)
20.	mov	R7,#4	@ Linux command code to write
21.	svc	0	@ Call Linux command.
22.			
23. @		Read input line from user keyboard or redirected file.	
24.			
25.	ldr	R1,=msg	@ Memory address to receive input
26.	mov	R0,#0	@ Stdin: Standard input (usually keyboard)
27.	mov	R7,#3	@ Linux command code to read
28.	mov	R2,#20	@ Maximum length to receive
29.	svc	0	@ Issue command to read.
30.			
31. @		Echo line just input back to the user one character at a time.	
32.			
33.	mov	R5,R0	@ Save a copy to test for exit.
34. inloop:	disp	v_bin1,tab	@ Display next character in binary.
35.	disp	v_hex1,tab	@ Display character in hexadecimal, then tab.
36.	disp	v_ascl,newln	@ Display character in ASCII, then line feed.
37.	add	R1,#1	@ Set address to next character in buffer.
38.	subs	R0,#1	@ Decrement number of characters remaining.
39.	bgt	inloop	@ Continue loop until message complete.
40.			
41. @		Go get another line, but exit if only "Enter" key was input.	
42.			
43.	cmp	R5,#1	@ Test if only the line feed character.

44.	bgt	_start	@ Loop back around to get another input.
45.	mov	R7,#1	@ Command 1 terminates programs.
46.	mov	R0,#0	@ Set exit code to zero.
47.	svc	0	@ Return full control to Linux.
48.			
49.	.data		
50. msg:	.ds	10	@ Memory buffer for keyboard input
51. prompt:	.ascii	"Please enter text message: "	
52. newln:	.ascii	"\n"	@ Line feed character code
53. tab:	.ascii	"\t"	@ Horizontal tab character code
54.	.end		

Listing 5.5: Subroutine to output binary number in ASCII

Listing 5.6 shows both the model.s and v_hex1.s source files being edited and compiled. The v_asc1 and v_bin1 subroutines have not been changed, so their object modules do not need to be updated. The linker command now includes five files: the executable "model" file as well as the four object files.

```
~$ nano model.s
~$ as -o model.o model.s
~$ nano v_hex1.s
~$ as -o v_hex1.o v_hex1.s
~$ ld -o model model.o v_asc1.o v_bin1.o v_hex1.o
~$ ./model
Please enter text message: Hi there
01001000        48        H
01101001        69        i
00100000        20
01110100        74        t
01101000        68        h
01100101        65        e
01110010        72        r
01100101        65        e
00100001        21        !
00001010        0A

Please enter text message:

~$
```

Listing 5.6: Program displaying binary, hexadecimal, and ASCII

— 6 —

ARM Machine Code

Assembly language programming provides a good hands-on introduction to computer architecture. Chapter 6 will describe the various components of an ARM processor machine code instruction. Modifications will be made to subroutines v_bin1 and v_hex1 to showcase some special features of the ARM instruction format.

Advanced RISC Machine (ARM)

Computers have never been fast enough. Application developers and users always want better performance, and electronics designers have generally been able to fulfill those expectations for decades. Of course, whenever one application is satisfied, another one that was previously "impossible" whets the appetite of application developers for continued performance enhancements. "Moore's Law" implies that computer performance will double every 18 months, mostly due to improvements in the packing density of transistors on integrated circuits. Oddly enough, this has proven to be the case for over three decades, far longer than many of us thought possible.

Not all of the performance improvements over the years have come from improvements in the structure of integrated circuits. Some have come from improvements in CPU design as well as running operations in parallel. As was presented in Chapter 1, most instructions executed by a CPU have the following four components:

- Op code
- Location to receive result
- Location of first operand
- Value or location of second operand

This format is popular because applications generally need computers to evaluate "binary operations" such as C=A+B, where addition is just one of the many arithmetic and logical operations having two operands. So where are these ABC variables located? Today, our computer systems have billions of bytes of storage in memory, but only about a couple dozen registers. Obviously, our variables are stored in main memory and only temporarily copied into the registers when we are using them in calculations. Figure 6.1 illustrates the general format of CPU instructions that was becoming popular around 1980. These instructions allowed the first operand (A in C=A+B example) to come from either a register or memory. The value for the second operand (B) could come from a register, memory, or be an immediate constant, such as C=A+6. The result of the calculation (C) could then be placed into a register or written into main memory.

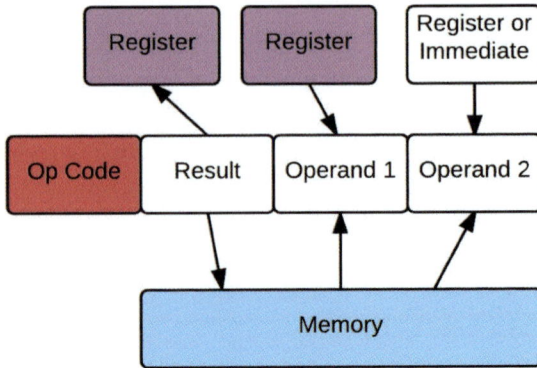

Figure 6.1: Instruction format in a CISC architecture

This instruction format actually enables C=A+B to be performed in a single CPU instruction and not even use any registers. The problem was one of execution speed, and it was being addressed in the early 1980s at the University of California, Berkeley, and Stanford University. The conclusion was to develop Reduced Instruction Set Computer (RISC) architectures. The primary difference between a RISC architecture and what was later referred to as a Complex Instruction Set Computer (CISC) architecture was that most instructions would only access data in registers, not in main memory. This difference accelerates program execution in two ways: the instructions are simpler in format thereby being easier to decode and of course getting data from registers is always faster than getting data from main memory.

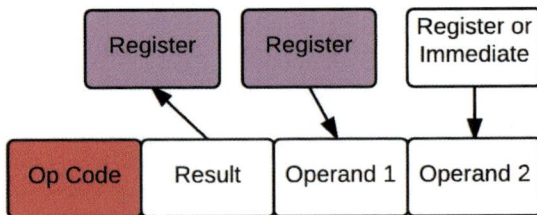

Figure 6.2: Instruction format in a RISC architecture

Obviously, variables in main memory will have to be accessed eventually, but optimizing program segments to keep as much data in registers as long as possible does lead to faster program executions. The second obvious point is that there has to be at least a few of instructions to access main memory: one to load registers and one to store register contents into memory. So, what does this have to do with the ARM processor in particular? Inspired by the research into RISC architectures, the British computer manufacturer, Acorn Computers, developed the Acorn RISC Machine (ARM), later renamed as the Advanced RISC Machine. With the exception of a few of memory load/store instructions, the ARM instruction format is very similar to that illustrated in Figure 6.2, but with an additional twist which we'll examine later in the chapter. There are actually several variations of the ARM architecture. In this book, we are working with the design present in the Raspberry Pi and Beaglebone Black computers, which currently contain the Cortex-A7 and Cortex-A8 formats, respectively.

Was this idea of a RISC architecture new in the mid 1980s? No, of course not. It was more a time of getting back to basics. Over a decade earlier, I was developing hardware/software applications for the supercomputer of that day: the Control Data CDC6600. Much of the speed of programs running on the CDC6600 came from CPU instructions that performed all ALU operations only in registers. Do all computers today have a RISC architecture? No. The one area where RISC architectures, and the ARM in particular, do have a monopoly is in portable devices like cell phones and tablets. RISC machines typically get much better throughput for the same amount of energy consumed, thereby getting much longer life from a battery charge.

Fetch, Decode, Execute

Almost all CPUs have the following three general stages for processing every instruction:

1. Fetch: Load next instruction from memory.
2. Decode: Break instruction into components: opcode, operands, flag ...
3. Execute: Do the actual work (add, logical and, shift, ...)

Thumb Machine Code

Although the ARM machine code instructions are 32 bits, there exists an alternate "Thumb" mode that squeezes instructions into a 16-bit format. Thumb is not a separate processor, but instead there are two different decode sections within the ARM CPU: one expecting instructions in 32-bit ARM format, and the alternate expecting instructions in Thumb format.

How does the ARM CPU know the difference between regular ARM instructions and Thumb instructions? If the T-bit (CPSR bit 5) is set to 1, the CPU assumes the PC register (Program Counter) is pointing to a Thumb format instruction, while if the T-bit is zero, the instruction is assumed to be a 32-bit

ARM instruction.

Are the Thumb instructions a subset of the set of ARM instructions? This is close to being true, but not exactly true. Most of the Thumb instructions are a limited version of corresponding 32-bit ARM instructions. What is the advantage of using the Thumb set of instructions? Performance, sometimes. Because Thumb instructions are only 16-bits wide, they take up less room in memory and will load faster in hardware configurations having a 16-bit data bus or smaller. Today's configurations, having 32-bit data buses and large memories, could actually run slower in Thumb-coded programs due to the Thumb's lack of features present in the full 32-bit ARM format as well as the overhead due to switching between ARM and Thumb modes.

I'm using the Thumb format to introduce ARM machine code instruction format due to its simplicity. There are no coding examples in this book using Thumb code.

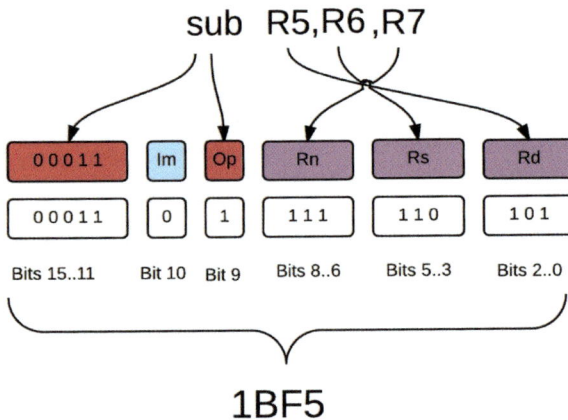

Figure 6.3: Thumb add/subtract machine code example

Take note of a few features of the Thumb add/subtract machine code instruction format illustrated in Figure 6.3

- Bits 11-15 indicate this is an add/subtract operation.
- Bit 9 indicates whether it is add (0) or subtract (1).
- Three registers can be used. In the example, [R6] is added to [R7] and the result is stored in R5.
- Only registers R0 through R7 can be used because only three bits in the instruction are allocated for each of the three registers.
- Bit 10 is the "immediate" flag. Figure 6.4 shows it being set, but the range of immediate values is only 0 through 7 (3 bits).

Assembly Language Coding in Color

sub R5,R6 ,#7

00011	Im	Op	Offset	Rs	Rd
00011	1	1	111	110	101
Bits 15..11	Bit 10	Bit 9	Bits 8..6	Bits 5..3	Bits 2..0

1FF5

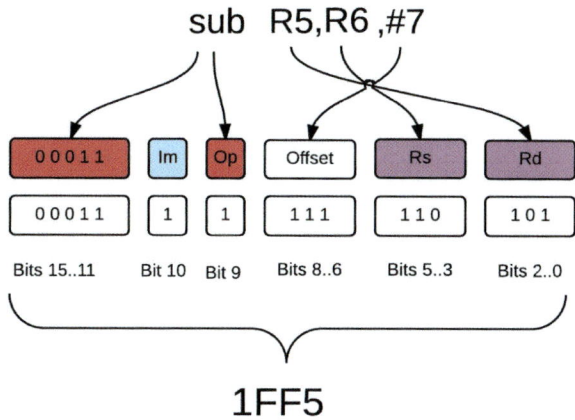

Figure 6.4: Thumb subtract with immediate data

ARM Machine Code

It's time to look behind the curtain. I've been hiding some of the complexity of the ARM instruction format until you got more comfortable working with assembly language.

- Most ARM instructions are conditionally executed (depends on the NZCV flags)
- Most ARM instructions have the option of modifying the NZCV flags
- Most ARM instructions can use four registers
- Most ARM instructions include a shift operation

Compared to almost every other CPU, the ARM architecture is very unique in how many instructions modify and check the condition flags of the CPSR:

1. Each data processing instruction has the option of whether to change the values of the NZCF flags or leave them as they were. On almost every other CPU design, arithmetic and logic functions (add, sub, and, or, …) always change the NZCV flags, and load/store instructions (mov, ldr, …) never change the NZCV flags.
2. Almost every ARM instruction can be conditionally executed depending on the value in the NZCF flags. Almost all other CPUs only have branch (also known as jump) instructions that examine the flags.

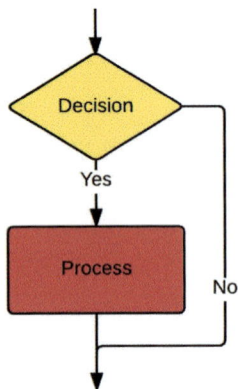

Figure 6.5: ARM instructions

ARM instructions are conditionally executed. Most computer architectures have a few instructions, such as JE (Jump if Equal) and JC (Jump if Carry), whose execution depends on the results from a previous instruction, but almost every ARM instruction can be set up to be "ignored" if a particular status condition is present. In other words, an ADD can be executed or ignored depending on the value of the status bits (carry, equal/zero, negative, overflow) that were set from the execution of a previous instruction.

In the ARM processor, the CPSR (Current Program Status Register) has N, Z, C, and V status flags:

N	Negative: Previous operation result was negative (i.e., bit 31 = 1)
Z	Zero: Previous operation result was zero (i.e., bits 31..0 = 0)
C	Carry: Previous operation resulted in a value that exceeded 32 bit register.
V	Overflow: Previous operation resulted in an error such as wrong positive/negative value.

Table 6.1: Status bits in the CPSR

Let's use the subtraction instruction as an example for showing the multiple formats available in the ARM:

sub	R1,R2	@ Subtract the value in R2 from R1, but do not change NZCV flags
subs	R1,R2	@ Subtract the value in R2 from R1, and change flags depending on the result
subeq	R1,R2	@ Like the first example, but only execute it if the Z-flag is set (i.e., a previous result was zero).
subeqs	R1,R2	@ Combination of previous two examples: only do the subtraction if the Z-flag is set, and also change NZCV based on subtraction results.

Listing 6.1: Subtraction instruction examples using status bits

Assembly Language Coding in Color

The ARM assembly language OpCode field, complete with conditional execution options, has the general format: **OpCode{cond}{s}**

1. The "OpCode" is simply the mnemonic for the operation to be performed by the current instruction (i.e., add, sub, mul. mov, …).
2. The "cond" is optional and indicates which combination of condition status bits has to be set (or clear) for the current instruction to be executed or ignored. Note: In the following list, "Z" means the Z-flag must be set (value=1), "!Z" means the Z-flag must be clear (value=0), "C" means the C-flag must be set, "!C" means the C-flag must be clear, etc.
3. The "s" is optional and indicates whether the NZCV condition status bits are to be modified by the execution of the current instruction.

EQ	Z	Equal (equals zero)
NE	!Z	Not equal
CS or HS	C	Carry set / unsigned higher or same
CC or LO	!C	Carry clear / unsigned lower
MI	N and !C	Minus / negative N set
PL	!N	Plus / positive or zero
VS	V	Overflow
VC	!V	No overflow
HI	!C and !Z	Unsigned higher
LS	!C or Z	Unsigned lower or same
GE	N = V	Signed greater than or equal
LT	N != V	Signed less than
GT	!Z and (N = V)	Signed greater than
LE	Z or (N != V)	Signed less than or equal
AL	Always (default)	Typically use blank (i.e., use b rather than bal)

Table 6.2: List of ARM assembly language condition codes

Although there is no single format that covers all ARM instructions, the following description covers the data processing instructions which include move (MOV), arithmetic (ADD, SUB, ...), and logical (AND, ORR, EOR) instructions. Note that all the shift instructions (LSL, …) are actually built into the move, arithmetic, and logical instructions and are not really individual instructions of their own.

Examine the following sequence of code that shows variations in the OpCodes which demonstrate the condition status flags use. It begins by loading initial values of 2 and 4 into registers R4 and R5, respectively.

mov	R5,#4	@ Always load: [R5] = 4 and do not change NZCV
mov	R4,#2	@ Always load: [R4] = 2 and do not change NZCV
subs	R5,R4	@ Always subtract: [R5] = [R5] − [R4] = 2 and change NZCV = 0000
moveq	R4,#10	@ Do nothing because Z=0 {ne}
subgts	R5,R4	@ Because Z=0 and N = V {gt}, subtract: [R5] = [R5] − [R4] = 0 and change NZCV = 0100
subeqs	R5,R4	@ Because Z=1 {eq}, subtract: [R5] = [R5] − [R4] = -2 and change NZCV = 1000
addmi	R5,R4	@ Because N=1 and C=0 {mi}, add: [R5] = [R5] + [R4] = 0 and leave NZCV unchanged
addne	R5,R4	@ Because Z=0 {ne}, do [R5] = [R5] + [R4] = 2 and leave NZCV unchanged

Listing 6.2: Sample code sequence that sets and tests status bits NZCV

Figure 6.6 and Table 6.3 show what the assembler must do to translate the format we enter as assembly language text to the binary format machine code required by the ARM processor.

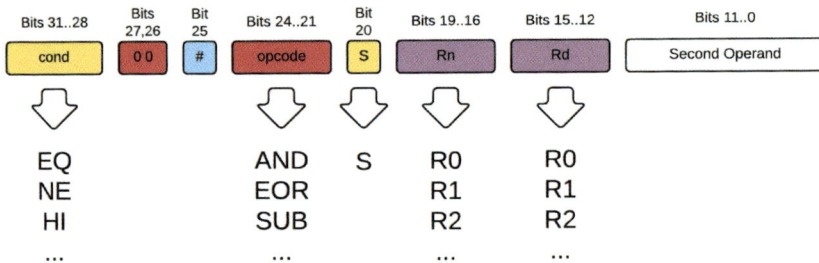

Figure 6.6: Assembler mnemonics mapped to positions in machine code

The machine code fields are filled with numbers associated with the above mnemonics. For example, EQ, NE, and HI are replaced by the binary numbers 0000, 0001, and 0010, respectively. The operations AND, EOR, and SUB are replaced by the binary opcode numbers 0000, 0001, and 0010, respectively. Obviously, register names such as R0, R1, and R2 are replaced by the binary numbers 0000, 0001, and 0010, respectively.

Assembly Language Coding in Color

bits	name	Contents
31..28	Cond	Only execute this instruction on condition of the value in the NZCF flags
27..26	00	These two bits are always zero for the data processing instruction type
25	#	Immediate operand flag
24..21	Opcode	Which operation (add, sub, and, orr, eor, ...)
20	S	Indicates that this instruction will modify the condition codes
19..16	Rn	ID number of register containing the minuend (first operand)
15..12	Rd	ID number of register to receive the result
11..0	op2	Three formats possible for second operand

Table 6.3: General bit layout for ARM data processing instructions (mov, add, sub, and, orr, eor, ...)

Let's continue to use the same subtraction example but include conditional assembly which is available in the 32-bit ARM instruction format. As before, we will subtract 7 from the contents of register R6, and store the result into register R5. However, in this example with the full power of the 32-bit ARM format, this instruction is only to be executed if the Z-flag is set, and its execution will set the NZCV flags depending on its result.

The assembler constructs the machine code instruction 0x02565007 by "filling in" the fields of the instruction word with "sub" = 0010, "eq" = 0000, "s" = 1, and "#" = 1. The operands and destination register ID are in the lower 20 bits of the instruction and consist of R5, R6, and the immediate constant of 7 as shown in the figure.

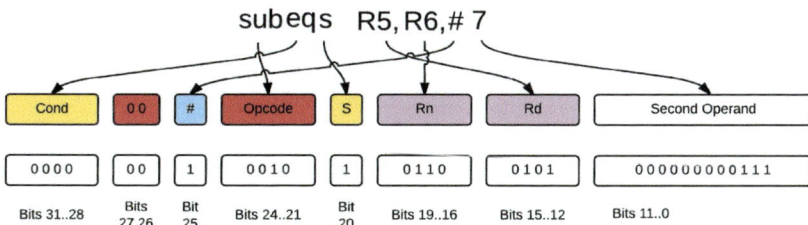

Figure 6.7: "Assemble" subtraction instruction to ARM machine code 0x02565007

The previous figure shows where the destination register (Rd) and first operand register (Rn) are located within the machine code format, but I've been somewhat vague about the second operand which can have a rather complicated format in itself. Even the immediate value (given as 7 in the illustration) is more complicated than it appears to be.

In general, a subtraction instruction looks like the following algebra:

$D = N - M \times 2^S$ where 2^S is not really an exponent, but a shift count.

- **D**: Destination register to hold the 32-bit result
- **N**: First operand register: In subtraction, it is the minuend (quantity from which another quantity is to be subtracted)
- **M×2^S**: Second operand: In subtraction, it is the subtrahend (quantity to subtract). There are three possible formats for M and S:
    1. **M** and **S** are both in registers: The contents of register M are shifted (logical, algebraic, or circular) by the value in register S.
    2. **M** is a register and **S** is a constant: The contents of register M are shifted (logical, algebraic, or circular) by a constant (range of 0 through 31).
    3. **M** and **S** are both constants: This is somewhat like scientific notation where M is a constant (0 through 255) and S is a shift count (0 through 30, even integers).

AND R1,R4,R3,LSR R6

Now let's demonstrate the full power of the ARM 32-bit data processing instruction format by replacing three instructions from subroutine v_bin with just one.

nxtbit:	mov	R1,R3	@ Copy byte to be displayed to R1.
	lsr	R1,R6	@ Shift current bit to bit 0.
	and	R1,#1	@ Mask off all bits except bit 0.
nxtbit:	and	R1,R4,R3,LSR R6	@ Select next 0 or 1 to display.

Listing 6.3: Replace three instructions from subroutine v_bin1 in Listing 5.1 with one AND instruction.

You're probably saying, "Wait a minute. That AND instruction looks pretty complicated." I've heard comments like, "I thought the ARM processor has a RISC (Reduced Instruction Set Computer) architecture containing a relatively small number of instructions, and those instructions are relatively simple compared to those of a CISC (Complex Instruction Set Computer) architecture. That AND instruction doesn't appear to be so simple."

If you thought the ARM was unique in the way it handles the setting and testing of the condition status bits, just look at how it works on most of its arithmetic and logic operations. First, didn't we already use the AND in Chapter

5, and didn't it use only one register and an immediate value? Didn't it work by doing a bit-by-bit logical "and" and leave the result in a register? That format which we used in Chapter 5 is the format of the AND used on almost every CPU manufactured in the past 50 years. Why and how does the ARM's AND use four registers? Also, what's that shift instruction doing inside the AND instruction? Take note: It's not just the AND that works this way, it's almost all the arithmetic and logical instructions.

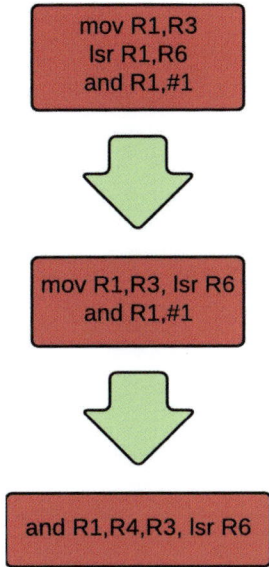

```
mov R1,R3
lsr R1,R6
and R1,#1
```

```
mov R1,R3, lsr R6
and R1,#1
```

```
and R1,R4,R3, lsr R6
```

Figure 6.8: Three instructions reduced to one

We will replace three instructions with one. These instructions were used to select a particular bit within the byte, shift it all the way to the right, and mask off all other bits so that it is by itself.

1. The first two instructions can be combined. All data processing instructions can have a buit-in shift included.
2. The next reduction requires another register to be preloaded with the mask. If R4 is preloaded with #1, then all three previous instructions are now combined into one.

In the following layout of the AND instruction, the op-code for AND = 0000, condition code "always" = 1110, "s" = 0, "#" = 0, and the LSR shift code is 01.

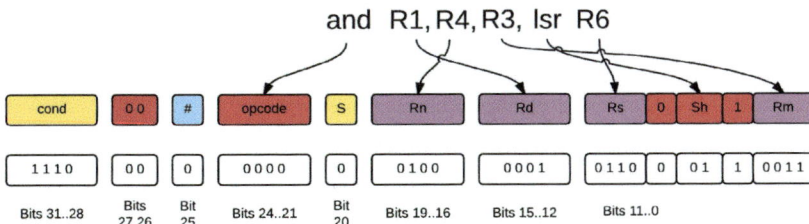

and R1, R4, R3, lsr R6

cond	0 0	#	opcode	S	Rn	Rd	Rs	0	Sh	1	Rm

1110	00	0	0000	0	0100	0001	0110	0	01	1	0011

| Bits 31..28 | Bits 27,26 | Bit 25 | Bits 24..21 | Bit 20 | Bits 19..16 | Bits 15..12 | Bits 11..0 |

Figure 6.9: Machine code generated by assembler

6: ARM Machine Code

Here's what that one "AND   R1,R4,R3,LSR R6" instruction does:

1. First, it takes the value from register R3 and shifts it right the number of bit positions specified in register R6.
2. Then, it combines that shifted value with the contents of register R4 using a Boolean "and" function.
3. And finally, it stores the result into register R1. The contents of registers R3, R4, and R6 are unchanged.

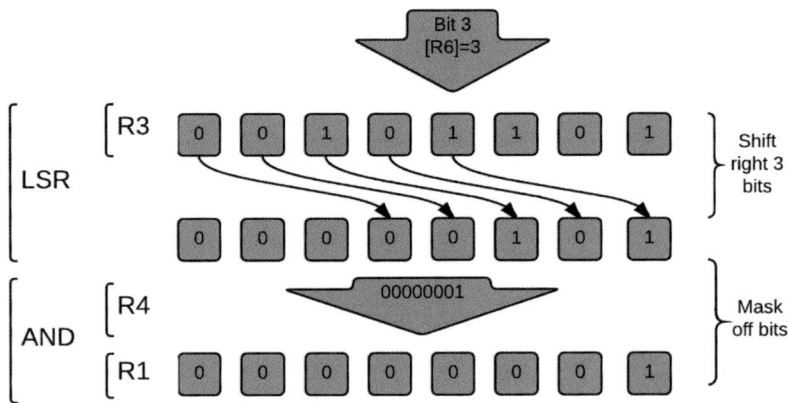

Figure 6.10: AND R1,R4,R3,LSR R6

So what's this one instruction really doing (i.e., why is it doing it)? It's selecting a single bit from R3 and putting it into the rightmost bit position in R1.

1. Not only is R6 counting down the number of passes through the loop, but it also points to the next bit to be displayed. For the first pass through the loop, [R6]=7. This 7 indicates there are 7 more passes through the loop It also indicates that bit 7 (the leftmost bit of a byte) will be displayed on this first pass through the loop. For the last pass through the loop, [R6] is 0. The R3 LSR R6 portion of the instruction simply shifts the desired bit into the rightmost position (bit 0).
2. Because R4 contains only a binary 1, the AND portion of the instruction masks off all bits except for the rightmost bit.
3. The result of the shift with AND is then stored in a separate register, R1, so that the working registers R3, R4, and R6 are not changed and will be ready for the next pass through the loop.

Assembly Language Coding in Color

```
 1.@        Subroutine v_bin1 displays one byte from memory in binary.
 2.@                R1: Points to byte in memory
 3.@                LR: Contains the return address
 4.@                All register contents will be preserved.
 5.
 6.        .global    v_bin1              @ Externalize the entry address.
 7.
 8. v_bin1:  push    {R0-R6,LR}          @ Save registers R0 through R6, LR.
 9.         ldrb     R3,[R1]             @ Load byte to be displayed.
10.         mov      R4,#1               @ Used to mask off 1 bit at a time
11.         ldr      R5,=dig             @ Pointer to "01" ASCII string
12.         mov      R6,#7               @ Bit 7 will be output first.
13.
14.@        Loop through each bit outputing it to the standard output display.
15.
16. nxtbit:  and     R1,R4,R3,LSR R6     @ Select next 0 or 1 to display.
17.         add      R1,R5               @ Set R1 pointing to "0" or "1"
18.         bl       v_asc1              @ Display "0" or "1".
19.         subs     R6,#1               @ Decrement number of bits to display
20.         bge      nxtbit              @ Go display next bit until all 8 displayed
21.
22.         pop      {R0-R6,LR}          @ Restore saved register contents
23.         bx       LR                  @ Return to the calling program
24.
25. dig:    .ascii   "01"                @ ASCII string of binary digits 0 and 1
26.         .end
```

Listing 6.4: New version of subroutine v_bin1 with new AND instruction

Table 6.4 shows the AND instruction selecting each bit from a 0b00101101 sample data value as R6 is decremented from 7 to 0 through the loop.

R6	R3 lsr R6	R1
7	0	0
6	0	0
5	1	1
4	10	0
3	101	1
2	1011	1
1	10110	0
0	101101	1

Table 6.4: AND instruction selects bit to be displayed

Subroutine v_hex1 can be upgraded in the same way where one instruction replaces three. The mask in register R4 will be a binary 1111 for a hexadecimal digit. Go ahead and reassemble files v_bin1.s and v_hex1.s, link them same as before, and verify that the results are the same.

```
 1. @           Subroutine v_hex1 displays one byte in hexadecimal.
 2. @                     R1: Points to byte in memory
 3. @                     LR: Contains the return address
 4. @                     All register contents will be preserved.
 5.
 6.        .global  v_hex1              @ Externalize the entry address.
 7.
 8. v_hex1:  push  {R1-R6,LR}          @ Save registers R0 through R7.
 9.          ldrb  R3,[R1]             @ Load byte to be displayed.
10.          mov   R4,#0b1111          @ Used to mask off 4 bits at a time
11.          ldr   R5,=dig             @ Pointer to "01" ASCII string
12.          mov   R6,#4               @ Bit 4 will be output first.
13.
14. @           Loop through groups of 4-bit nibbles and output each to stdout.
15.
16. nxthex:  and   R1,R4,R3,LSR R6     @ Select next hex digit (0 .. F).
17.          add   R1,R5               @ Set R1 pointing to "0", "1", ... or "F"
18.          bl    v_asc1              @ Linux command code to write string.
19.          subs  R6,#4               @ Decrement number of bits to display
20.          bge   nxthex              @ Go display next nibble
21.
22.          pop   {R1-R6,LR}          @ Restore saved register contents
23.          bx    LR                  @ Return to the calling program
24.
25. dig:     .ascii "0123456789"       @ ASCII string of digits 0 through 9
26.          .ascii "ABCDEF"           @ ASCII string of digits A through F
27.          .end
```

Listing 6.5: New version of subroutine v_hex1 with new AND instruction

Is there anything else I'm hiding? Well, it's not the end of the book. Is it? As far as the standard ARM instructions go, there won't be many more surprises, but we do have upcoming complexity in moving data between registers and memory. Actually, all this stuff is pretty easy once you know it, but so is swimming or driving an automobile.

— 7 —
Memory Access

The focus of the preceding chapters has been on instructions using data already in registers. In Chapter 7, we will lean more toward the details of data formats and the instructions that move data between registers and memory.

Bits, Bytes, Words

How many bits does one machine code instruction move between the registers and memory? In the ARM processor, that number depends on the type of load/store instruction and varies between 8 and 512 bits. Note: This is the number of bits moved by one instruction, but not necessarily in one clock cycle. The following load/store instructions are available:

- 1 byte (8 bits): LDRB, LDRSB, STRB
- 1 half word (16 bits): LDRH, LDRSH, STRH
- 1 word (32 bits): LDR, STR
- 1 to 16 words (between 32 and 512 bits): LDM, STM

Operation	Number of bits stored	Bit position in registers
STR	32 bits (1 word)	Bits 0 to 31 (whole register)
STRB	8 bits (1 byte)	Bits 0 to 7 (right side)
STRH	16 bits (1 half word)	Bits 0 to 15 (right half register)
STM	Between 32 and 512 bits (1 to 16 words)	All 32 bits of each of the selected registers

Table 7.1: Operations that store data into memory from registers

All 16 ARM general purpose registers, R0 through R15, have 32 bits. Table 7.1 indicates that the instructions that store a partial register (STRB, STRH) copy the low order bits to memory. The high order bits of the register (bits 31-8 for STRB and bits 31-16 for STRH) are not copied into memory.

Operation	Number of bits loaded	Bit position in registers
LDR	32 bits (1 word)	Bits 0 to 31 (whole register)
LDRB	8 bits (1 byte)	Bits 0 to 7 (right side), zero fill bits 8 to 31
LDRSB	8 bits (1 byte)	Bits 0 to 7, sign extend bits 8 to 31
LDRH	16 bits (1 half word)	Bits 0 to 15 (right half register), zero fill bits 16 to 31
LDRSH	16 bits (1 half word)	Bits 0 to 15, sign extend bits 16 to 31
LDM	Between 32 and 512 bits (1 to 16 words)	All 32 bits of each of the selected registers

Table 7.2: Operations that load data from memory into registers

In the partial register store instructions, the high order bits of the register are ignored. Are they also ignored in the corresponding partial register load instructions? No. The high order bits are either set to zero (LDRB, LDRH), or they are filled with the sign bit. For LDRSB, bit 7 of the byte in memory will not only be copied into bit 7 of the register, but also bits 8 through 31 of the register. For the half-word load (LDRHS), the same bit loaded into bit 15 of the register will also be copied into bits 16 through 31. In other words, the sign of the byte or half-word in memory will be the sign of the data loaded into the register.

Arrays, Tables, Vectors, Matrices

An array is an ordered list of adjacent storage locations in memory. It could be a list of bytes, words, or even a more complicated combination of bytes and words. Tables, vectors, and matrices are other names commonly associated with arrays, and many times only differ by the number of dimensions (number of rows, number of columns, etc.). A register is typically used to "index" into an array as well as sequentially step through each value from the beginning to the end.

```
dig:    .ascii    "0123456789"    @ ASCII string of digits 0 through 9
        .ascii    "ABCDEF"        @ ASCII string of digits A through F
```

Listing 7.1: Example of byte array containing characters

Base Registers

On most computer systems, instructions that load or store data into memory generate the absolute memory address from the addition of the contents of a base register plus some offset contained within the instruction. In the ARM architecture, any of the registers R0 through R15 can be used as a base register in an instruction. Remember that R13, R14, and R15 are also used as the stack pointer SP, link register LR, and program counter PC, respectively.

Indexed Addressing

There are three addressing modes in the ARM for moving data between a single register and a memory location:

- Indirect: The base register contains the complete memory address. Example: LDRB R3,[R1].
- Pre-Indexed: The base register is first updated by adding an immediate constant to it before it provides the memory address for the current instruction. Example: STRB R2,[R4,#1].
- Post-Indexed: The base register contains the complete memory address, but then the base register contents will be updated by adding an immediate constant to it after the address is used in the current instruction. Example: STRB R05,[R4],#-1.

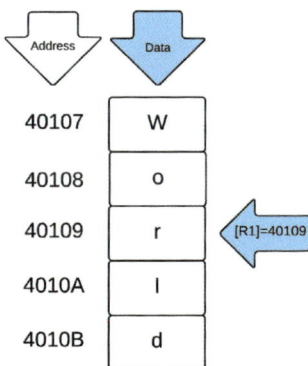

Figure 7.1 illustrates the indirect mode where register R1 contains the memory address all by itself. This mode is shown on line 10 of the following v_dig1 subroutine.

Figure 7.1: Register R1 points to memory location

It's easy to remember which assembler syntax distinguishes "pre" from "post" because it is similar to common algebraic expressions. The brackets enclose what is to be done first. In A×[B+56], we add B and 56 before (pre) using it to multiply by A. While in [A×B]+56, we first multiply A and B, and next we add 56 (post). Likewise, [R4,#1] is pre-indexed addressing, and [R4],#-1 is post-indexed addressing.

Display in Any Base

Subroutine v_dig1 is written to demonstrate the use of indexed load and store instructions. Its function is similar to that of subroutines v_bin1 and v_hex1, except it can display a number in any base between 2 and 16. The upper limit of base 16 is only because the symbol table (array dig) stops at the letter F, and no higher bases are in common use anyway.

Program flow of subroutine v_dig1:

1. Build a table of powers of the selected base: If X is the base (contained in R0), then it starts with X^0 followed by X^1, X^2, etc. For example, in base ten this will be 1, 10, 100. For base two, it will be 1, 2, 4, 8, 16, etc.
2. Loop to calculate the digits for each column: This is actually a nested loop where the outer loop indexes through the power table built in the previous step, and the inner loop performs a "divide" using repeated subtraction. Note: The ARM processor has no divide instruction, so the equivalent of division is calculated by repeated subtraction.
3. Calculate the least significant digit ("one's" column): This rightmost digit is calculated by a simple addition to get the pointer to the correct digit.

```
 1. @          Subroutine v_dig1 displays one byte in a selected base.
 2. @                       R0: Contains the base (2 through 16)
 3. @                       R1: Points to byte in memory
 4. @                       LR: Contains the return address
 5. @                       All register contents will be preserved.
 6.
 7.            .global    v_dig1        @ Externalize the entry address.
 8.
 9. v_dig1:    push       {R1-R5,LR}    @ Save registers R1 to R5, LR.
10.            ldrb       R3,[R1]       @ Load byte to be displayed.
11.            cmp        R3,R0         @ Only one's column is needed?
12.            blt        onecol        @ Go output "only" column of display.
13.
14. @          Build power table for base: X**0, X**1, X**2, ...
15.
16.            ldr        R4,=power     @ Point to power table in memory.
```

17.	mov	R2,R0	@ Copy the base to begin with X**1.
18. initb:	strb	R2,[R4,#1]!	@ Store next power of base.
19.	mul	R2,R0	@ Calculate next power of base.
20.	cmp	R2,R3	@ Check if reached power-of-base needed.
21.	ble	initb	@ Continue until enough digits reached.
22.			
23. @		Loop back through power table and output digit for each column.	
24.			
25. nxtdig:	ldr	R1,=dig-1	@ Point to 1 "0123456789ABCDEF" string
26.	ldrb	R5,[R4],#-1	@ Load next lower power (i.e., column)
27.			
28. @		Calculate next digit to be displayed.	
29.			
30. modX:	add	R1,#1	@ Set R1 pointing to next higher digit.
31.	subs	R3,R5	@ Count down to find the correct digit.
32.	bge	modX	@ Keep subtracting current column value.
33.	addlt	R3,R5	@ We counted one too many (went negative)
34.	bl	v_asc1	@ R1 points to 1 ASCII character to display.
35.	cmp	R5,R0	@ Test if all the way to the one's column.
36.	bgt	nxtdig	@ If 1's column, go output it.
37.			
38. @		Finish multi-digit display by calculating the one's digit.	
39.			
40. onecol:	ldr	R1,=dig	@ Pointer to "0123456789"
41.	add	R1,R3	@ Generate offset into "0123456789".
42.	bl	v_asc1	@ Display one's column digit.
43.	pop	{R1−R5,LR}	@ Restore saved register contents
44.	bx	LR	@ Return to the calling program
45.			
46.	.data		
47. power:	.byte	1	@ Any non-zero number to the zeroth power.
48.	.ds	5	@ Reserve space for powers of base
49. dig:	.ascii	"0123456789"	@ ASCII string of digits 0 through 9
50.	.ascii	"ABCDEF"	@ ASCII string of digits A through F
51.	.end		

Listing 7.2: Subroutine v_dig1 displays in any base (2 through 16)

STRB R2,[R4,#1]!

On line 18 in Listing 7.2, the [R4,#1] expression indicates pre-indexed format, where the address of the byte to be stored is determined by the sum of the contents of base register R4 and immediate value 1. Although R4 is a register, I have color-coded [R4,#1] as blue in the listing because it points to a data address in memory. The exclamation point (!) indicates that the address generated by the sum of the base register and immediate offset will update the base register.

Figure 7.2 shows the machine code instruction that is generated by the assembler. How large of an immediate offset can be added to or subtracted from a base register in pre-indexed format?

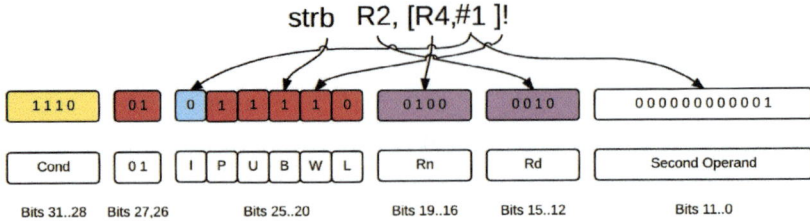

Figure 7.2: Machine code generated for pre-indexed mode store byte instruction

As seen in Figure 7.2, twelve bits are available in the second operand which provide a maximum immediate offset of 4095 bytes. The field definitions of the LDRB/STRB machine code instructions depicted in figures 7.2 and 7.3 are provided below:

- Cond (bits 31..28): Status indicating whether instruction should be executed (1110 indicates always execute).
- 0 1 (bits 27,26): Opcode indicating that this is an LDR/STR instruction.
- IPUBWL (bits 25..20): Bits indicating specifically what is to be done by LDR/STR instruction.
  - I (bit 25): "0" indicates offset is immediate (#) rather than register with shift.
  - P (bit 24): "1" indicates pre-indexed, "0" indicates post-indexed.
  - U (bit 23): "1" indicates up (add the offset), "0" indicates subtract the offset.
  - B (bit 22): "1" indicates byte (LDRB), "0" indicates word (LDR).
  - W (bit 21): "1" indicates write back (!), i.e. update the base register.
  - L (bit 20): "1" indicates load (LDR), "0" indicates store (STR).
- Rn (bits 19..16): Register to contain result, R0 through R15
- Rd (bits 15..12): Base register, R0 through R15
- Offset (bits 11..0): Immediate range of +4095 to -4095. This can also be in a register with a shift (see Figure 6.9).

Assembly Language Coding in Color

Please recall that R13, R14, and R15 are the stack pointer SP, link register LR, and program counter PC, respectively. Although using any of these three registers as a base register or result register can provide some clever results, use them carefully. For the Load Byte instruction, the 8 bit byte is loaded into the lower 8 bits, while the upper 24 bits will be set to zero.

As you recall from the format of the data processing instructions in Chapter 6, the second operand doesn't have to be an immediate constant, but instead can be a register with a shift. For example, the instruction "LDR R1, [R2,R3 LSR #2]" loads R1 from a word in an array whose beginning is pointed to by R2, and its "word position" is in R3. Since the ARM is byte-addressable, the word address must be multiplied by four, which is the same as shifting left two bit positions (LSR #2).

Figure 7.3 illustrates the machine code instruction generated for "LDRB R5, [R4],#-1" on line 26 which is a post-indexed instruction.

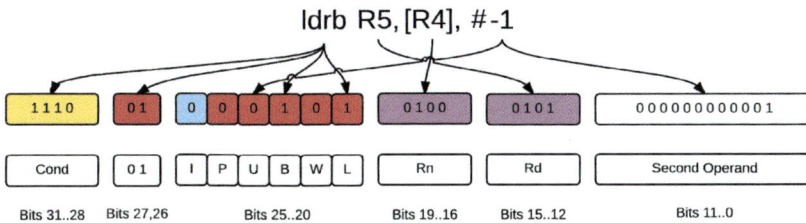

Figure 7.3: Machine code generated for post-indexed mode load byte instruction.

In post-indexed mode, the write-back option (!) to update the base register is not an option. The exclamation symbol is not allowed by the assembler since it is always implied. If an offset is present, such as either an immediate value or a register with a shift, it will be used to update the base register. It really would not make much sense to calculate a new index offset and not ever use it. I color-coded only the [R4] in blue and not the #-1 because the R4 contains the complete address, and the -1 "write back" to update R4 takes place after the data is loaded from memory. Perhaps the #-1 should have been color-code in red because it is a second operation that takes place within the instruction.

The model program is now being modified in Listing 7.3 to include the v_dig1 subroutine:

- Macro "dispbs" has been included on lines 15 through 26: It calls subroutine v_dig1 to display the numeric value of a byte of memory data pointed to by register R1.
- On line 49, the value of a byte of memory is displayed in decimal: Actually, subroutines v_bin1 and v_hex1 are no longer needed because their function can now be performed by v_dig1 even though it is much less efficient from an execution time viewpoint. For example, "disp v_hex1,tab" could be replaced by "dispbs 16,tab" on line 48.

1.	.global	_start	@ Program starting address for linker
2.			
3.@		Macro "disp sub,tail" calls a subroutine, then displays a character.	
4.@		sub: Subroutine to be called	
5.@		tail: Separation character to be output	
6.			
7.	.macro	disp	sub,tail
8.	bl	\sub	@ Call desired subroutine.
9.	push	{R1}	@ Save value that is in R1.
10.	ldr	R1,=\tail @ Separation character.	
11.	bl	v_asc1	@ Display single character.
12.	pop	{R1}	@ Restore original value in R1.
13.	.endm		
14.			
15.@		Macro "dispbs base, tail" calls v_dig1, then displays a character.	
16.@		base: Base (2 - 16) in which to display number	
17.@		tail: Separation character to be output	
18.			
19.	.macro	dispbs base ,tail	
20.	push	{R0,R1}	@ Save values from R0 and R1.
21.	mov	R0,#\base	@ Load base for display.
22.	bl	v_dig1	@ Display number in base ...
23.	ldr	R1,=\tail	@ Separation character.
24.	bl	v_asc1	@ Display single character.
25.	pop	{R0,R1}	@ Restore original values.
26.	.endm		
27.			
28.@		Display prompt message.	
29.			
30._start:	ldr	R1,=prompt	@ Load pointer to message.
31.	mov	R2,#27	@ Number of characters in message

```
32.         mov     R0,#1       @ Stdout: Standard output (usually monitor)
33.         mov     R7,#4       @ Linux command code to write
34.         svc     0           @ Call Linux command.
35.
36. @       Read input line from user keyboard or redirected file.
37.
38.         ldr     R1,=msg     @ Memory address to receive input
39.         mov     R0,#0       @ Stdin: Standard input (usually keyboard)
40.         mov     R7,#3       @ Linux command code to read
41.         mov     R2,#20      @ Maximum length to receive
42.         svc     0           @ Issue command to read.
43.
44. @       Echo line just input back to the user one character at a time.
45.
46.         mov     R5,R0       @ Save a copy to test for exit.
47. inloop: disp    v_bin1, tab @ Display in binary and tab separator.
48.         disp    v_hex1, tab @ Display hexadecimal and tab.
49.         dispbs  10, tab     @ Display character code in decimal.
50.         disp    v_asc1,newln @ Display in ASCII and line feed.
51.         add     R1,#1       @ Set address to next character in buffer.
52.         subs    R0,#1       @ Decrement number of characters
                                remaining.
53.         bgt     inloop      @ Continue loop until message complete.
54.
55. @       Go get another line, but exit if only "Enter" key was input.
56.
57.         cmp     R5,#1       @ Test if only the line feed character.
58.         bgt     _start      @ Loop back around to get another input.
59.         mov     R7,#1       @ Command 1 terminates programs.
60.         mov     R0,#0       @ Set exit code to zero.
61.         svc     0           @ Return full control to Linux.
62.
63.         .data
64. msg:    .ds     10          @ Memory buffer for keyboard input
65. prompt: .ascii  "Please enter text message: "
66. newln:  .ascii  "\n"        @ Line feed character code
67. tab:    .ascii  "\t"        @ Horizontal tab character code
68.         .end
```

Listing 7.3: Main program that echoes input line in multiple bases

Listing 7.4 shows subroutine v_dig1 being assembled and linked into the model program which also includes subroutines v_asc1, v_bin1, and v_hex1. The output now shows each character being echoed in binary, hexadecimal, decimal, and ASCII. If a different base, such as base 8 octal is desired, only the value on line 49 of the model.s source would have to be changed from a 10 (decimal) to an 8 (octal).

```
~$ nano v_dig1.s
~$ as -o v_dig1.o v_dig1.s
~$ nano model.s
~$ as -o model.o model.s
~$ ld -o model model.o v_asc1.o v_bin1.o v_hex1.o v_dig1.o
~$ ./model
Please enter text message: Hi there
01001000            48          72          H
01101001            69          105         i
00100000            20          32
01110100            74          116         t
01101000            68          104         h
01100101            65          101         e
01110010            72          114         r
01100101            65          101         e
00100001            21          33          !
00001010            0A          10

Please enter text message:

~$
```

Listing 7.4: Program displaying binary, hexadecimal, decimal, and ASCII

Case Conversion Example

We will now write a new program "vector" to showcase the STM (Store Multiple) and LDM (Load Multiple) instructions which move data between memory and multiple registers at a time. Instead of displaying each character one at a time, we'll modify the case of letters from the input buffer before echoing them on the display monitor. In the first example, only the first four letters in the buffer will be changed because only one word (4 bytes) will be modified.

In ASCII, the difference between the character code for a lower case letter and an upper case letter is bit 5. As shown in Figure 7.4, the upper case "A" can be changed to lower case by setting bit 5. This can either be done through addition or the inclusive OR (ORR instruction), both of which are commonly represented by the plus sign.

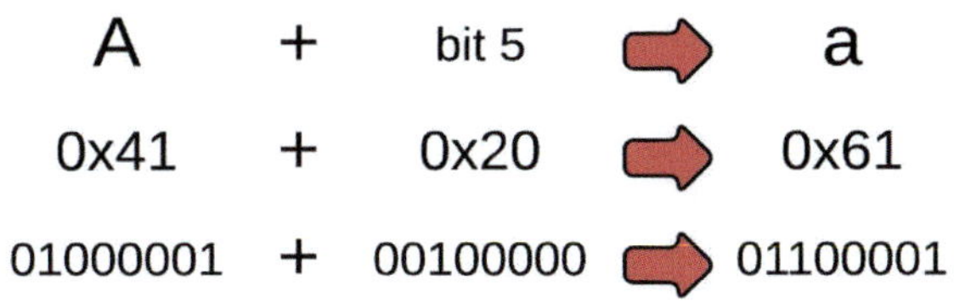

A	+	bit 5	➡	a
0x41	+	0x20	➡	0x61
01000001	+	00100000	➡	01100001

Figure 7.4: Convert upper case ASCII letter to lower case

The three logical operators available in almost every computer architecture are the AND, the inclusive OR, and the exclusive OR. Their truth tables, as well as the ARM operator names, are provided in Figure 7.5. We have already used the AND operation in previous examples, so we will now use the EOR (exclusive OR) to switch the case of letters and the ORR (inclusive OR) to force letters to lower case.

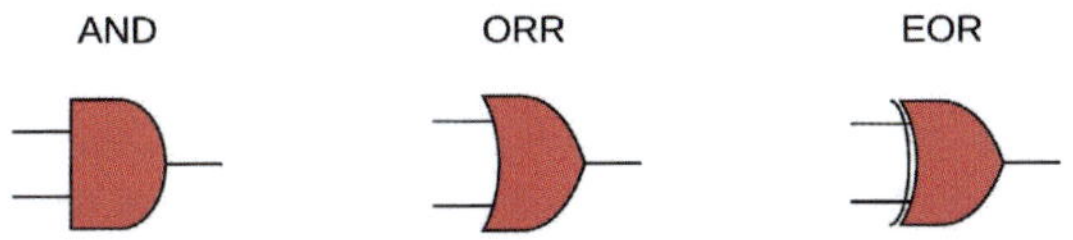

A	B	AND
0	0	0
0	1	0
1	0	0
1	1	1

A	B	ORR
0	0	0
0	1	1
1	0	1
1	1	1

A	B	EOR
0	0	0
0	1	1
1	0	1
1	1	0

Figure 7.5: Truth tables for the logical AND, OR, and exclusive OR operations

The vector program in Listing 7.5 is a stand-alone program without any subroutines. It performes the following:

1. Prompts the user and reads a text line from the keyboard.
2. Echoes the input line back to the user the same as it was received.
3. Toggles the "case" of the first four bytes, where lower case letters are converted to upper case, and upper case letters are converted to lower case. The entire text line will then be displayed. Warning: If non-alpha characters are in the first four bytes, unusual conversions may take place.
4. Convert the first four bytes to lower case. The entire text line will then be displayed again.
5. Continue the above four steps until a blank line is input.

1.		.global	_start	@ Program starting address for linker
2.				
3.	@	Display prompt message		
4.				
5.	_start:	ldr	R1,=prompt	@ Load pointer to message.
6.		mov	R2,#27	@ Number of characters in message
7.		mov	R0,#1	@ Stdout: Standard output (usually monitor)
8.		mov	R7,#4	@ Linux command code to write
9.		svc	0	@ Call Linux command.
10.				
11.	@	Read input line from user keyboard or redirected file.		
12.				
13.		ldr	R1,=msg	@ Memory address to receive input
14.		mov	R0,#0	@ Stdin: Standard input (usually keyboard)
15.		mov	R7,#3	@ Linux command code to read
16.		mov	R2,#30	@ Maximum length to receive
17.		svc	0	@ Issue command to read.
18.				
19.	@	Echo line just input back to the user.		
20.				
21.		mov	R2,R0	@ Number of characters input
22.		mov	R0,#1	@ Code for stdout (usually the monitor)
23.		mov	R7,#4	@ Linux service command code to write
24.		svc	0	@ Call Linux command.
25.				
26.	@	Change case of first 4 letters and echo again		
27.				
28.		ldr	R6,=cvt	@ Load pointer to 0x20202020
29.		ldr	R12,[R6]	@ Load 32-bit pattern into R12
30.		ldr	R8,[R1]	@ Load first 4 characters into R8.
31.		eor	R8,R8,R12	@ "Flip" the case of 4 letters.
32.		str	R8,[R1]	@ Overlay with changed case letters.

Assembly Language Coding in Color

```
33.      mov      R0,#1          @ [R0] = stdout (R1, R2, R7 still OK)
34.      svc      0              @ Call Linux command to display again.
35.
36. @    Convert to lower case and echo again
37.
38.      orr      R8,R8,R12      @ Convert 4 letters to lower case.
39.      str      R8,[R1]        @ Overlay with lower case letters.
40.      mov      R0,#1          @ [R0] = stdout (R1, R2, R7 still OK)
41.      svc      0              @ Call Linux command to display again.
42.
43. @    Go get another line, but exit if only "Enter" key input.
44.
45.      cmp      R2,#1          @ Test if only the line feed character.
46.      bgt      _start         @ Loop back around to get another input.
47.      mov      R7,#1          @ Command 1 terminates programs.
48.      mov      R0,#0          @ Set exit code to zero.
49.      svc      0              @ Return full control to Linux.
50.
51.      .data
52. cvt: .word    0x20202020     @ Pattern to convert letter case.
53. msg: .ds      15             @ Memory buffer for keyboard input
54. prompt: .ascii "Please enter text message: "
55.      .end
```

Listing 7.5: Vector program that changes the case of the first four letters input..

On lines 31 and 38, thirty-two logical operations take place simultaneously in bit-wise parallel operations. The EOR on line 31 takes the exclusive OR of bit 0 from registers R8 and R12, and places the result into bit 0 of register R8. The same thing is done for the other bit positions 1 through 31. Each bit in register R8 is EORed with its corresponding bit in register R12. Because R12 contains the pattern 0x20202020, the exclusive OR will toggle bit 5 of each of the four ASCII characters loaded into R8, thereby changing their cases. The inclusive OR on line 38 is similar, except it sets bit 5 of each of the four letters in R8, thereby setting them to lower case.

I could have only converted the first character in the text lines by using a STRB instruction instead of the full register STR, but I'm using this sample program to demonstrate multiple operations taking place simultaneously. We start here with four characters at a time, then move on to sixteen using the load and store multiple register commands. In Chapter 8, we will use the NEON coprocessor to even perform simultaneous logical operations on the equivalent of four 32-bit registers.

```
~$ as -o vector.o vector.s
~$ ld -o vector vector.o
~$ ./vector
Please enter text message: This is a test
This is a test
tHIS is a test
this is a test
Please enter text message: AbCdEfGhIjKlMnOp
AbCdEfGhIjKlMnOp
aBcDEfGhIjKlMnOp
abcdEfGhIjKlMnOp
Please enter text message:

~$
```

Listing 7.6: Assemble, link, and test execution of "vector" program.

Store and Load Multiple Registers

The contents of as many as sixteen registers can be moved to or from memory with one "block transfer" instruction. The STM (Store Multiple) and LDM (Load Multiple) instructions move data between memory and registers. We've actually used a subset of these before disguised as PUSH and POP. An example instruction is STMIA R8,{R0-R7} where R8 is the base register providing the indirect memory location, and the set of registers is identified within a pair of braces like {R0-R7}.

- All 32 bits of each register are always moved (i.e., no single bytes).
- A register must be specified as a "base register" which points to the memory address
- Obviously, not all registers will be moved within one memory clock cycle, but at least only one instruction needs to be executed.
- Any combination of from one to sixteen registers can be specified.
- The order of registers doesn't matter as each of the following examples selects the same set of registers: R1,R2,R3,R5,R6, and R7.
  - {R1-R3,R5-R7}
  - {R6,R2,R7,R3,R5,R1}
  - {R6-R7,R5,R1-R3}

The term "block transfer" in the ARM architecture is different than its meaning in most CPUs, where it refers to copying multiple bytes of data from one location in memory to another. In the ARM, it refers to the group of eight load and store multiple instructions. Each instruction's name is built from three parts shown in Figure 7.6.

Load Multiple (ldm)	Increment (i)	Before (b)
Store Multiple (stm)	Decrement (d)	After (a)

Figure 7.6: Three parts of the block transfer instructions

- ldmib: Load Multiple Increment Before
- ldmia: Load Multiple Increment After
- ldmdb: Load Multiple Decrement Before
- ldmda: Load Multiple Decrement After
- stmib: Store Multiple Increment Before
- stmia: Store Multiple Increment After
- stmdb: Store Multiple Decrement Before
- stmda: Store Multiple Decrement After

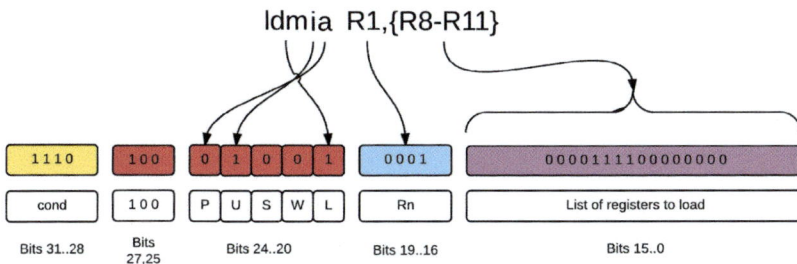

Figure 7.7: Sample data to describe block transfer

Figure 7.7 provides the machine code format of a load multiple register instruction. Notice how the list of registers to be loaded fills the lower 16 bits. Figure 7.8 is similar except it illustrates different options for the same type of instruction.

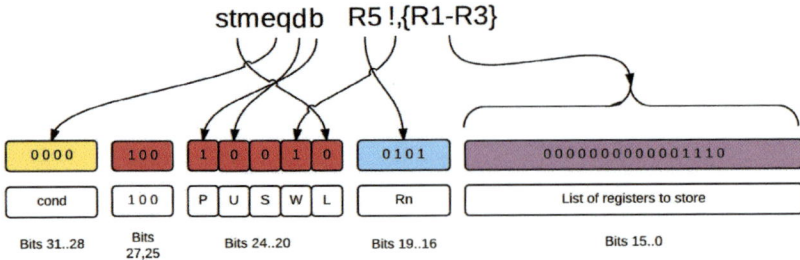

Figure 7.8: Block transfer with write-back and conditional execution

The load and store multiple instructions are similar in structure to data processing instructions, except there is a register list as a second operand:

- Cond (bits 31..28): Status indicating whether instruction should be executed (1110 indicates always).
- 1 0 0 (bits 27..25): Opcode indicating that this is a LDM/STM instruction.
- PUSWL (bits 24..20): Bits indicating specifically what is to be done by LDM/STM instruction.
    - P (bit 24): "1" indicates pre-indexed (before), "0" indicates post-indexed (after).
    - U (bit 23): "1" indicates increment address, "0" indicates decrement address.
    - S (bit 22): special use only by operating system .
    - W (bit 21): "1" indicates write-back, i.e., update the base register, "0" indicates no update.
    - L (bit 20): "1" indicates load from memory (LDM), "0" indicates store (STM).
- Rn (bits 19..16): Indicates which register (R0 through R15) is used as base register.
- List (bits 15..0): Indicates which registers (R0 through R15) are loaded/stored.

As you might expect, all the multiple load/store instructions can be conditionally executed as the example in Figure 7.8 shows. The other thing you probably suspect is that the base register can be updated using the exclamation point.

Assembly Language Coding in Color

The following listing shows the vector program updated to modify the case of the first 16 letters that are input. All four words, containing four bytes each, are loaded with one instruction on line 30. It takes four EOR instructions to convert the total of 16 bytes. This will be reduced to one NEON instruction in the next chapter. All 16 bytes are then stored back into memory with one multiple word store instruction on line 35.

1.	.global	_start	@ Program starting address for linker
2.			
3. @	Display prompt message		
4.			
5. _start:	ldr	R1,=prompt	@ Load pointer to message.
6.	mov	R2,#27	@ Number of characters in message
7.	mov	R0,#1	@ Stdout: Standard output (usually monitor)
8.	mov	R7,#4	@ Linux command code to write
9.	svc	0	@ Call Linux command.
10.			
11. @	Read input line from user keyboard or redirected file.		
12.			
13.	ldr	R1,=msg	@ Memory address to receive input
14.	mov	R0,#0	@ Stdin: Standard input (usually keyboard)
15.	mov	R7,#3	@ Linux command code to read
16.	mov	R2,#30	@ Maximum length to receive
17.	svc	0	@ Issue command to read.
18.			
19. @	Echo line just input back to the user.		
20.			
21.	mov	R2,R0	@ Number of characters input
22.	mov	R0,#1	@ Code for stdout (usually the monitor)
23.	mov	R7,#4	@ Linux service command code to write
24.	svc	0	@ Call Linux command.
25.			
26. @	Change case of first 16 letters and echo again		
27.			
28.	ldr	R6,=cvt	@ Load pointer to 0x20202020
29.	ldr	R12,[R6]	@ Load 32-bit pattern into R12
30.	ldmia	R1,{R8-R11}	@ Load first 16 characters input
31.	eor	R8,R8,R12	@ "Flip" the case of 4 letters.
32.	eor	R9,R9,R12	@ "Flip" the case of 4 letters.
33.	eor	R10,R10,R12	@ "Flip" the case of 4 letters.
34.	eor	R11,R11,R12	@ "Flip" the case of 4 letters.
35.	stmia	R1,{R8-R11}	@ Overlay with changed case letters.
36.	mov	R0,#1	@ [R0] = stdout (R1, R2, R7 still OK)
37.	svc	0	@ Call Linux command to display again.
38.			
39. @	Convert to lower case and echo again		

40.			
41.	orr	R8,R8,R12	@ Convert 4 letters to lower case.
42.	orr	R9,R9,R12	@ Convert 4 letters to lower case.
43.	orr	R10,R10,R12	@ Convert 4 letters to lower case.
44.	orr	R11,R11,R12	@ Convert 4 letters to lower case.
45.	stmia	R1,{R8-R11}	@ Overlay with lower case letters.
46.	mov	R0,#1	@ [R0] = stdout (R1, R2, R7 still OK)
47.	svc	0	@ Call Linux command to display again.
48.			
49. @		Go get another line, but exit if only "Enter" key input.	
50.			
51.	cmp	R2,#1	@ Test if only the line feed character.
52.	bgt	_start	@ Loop back around to get another input.
53.	mov	R7,#1	@ Command 1 terminates programs.
54.	mov	R0,#0	@ Set exit code to zero.
55.	svc	0	@ Return full control to Linux.
56.			
57.	.data		
58. cvt:	.word	0x20202020	@ Pattern to convert letter case.
59. msg:	.ds	15	@ Memory buffer for keyboard input
60. prompt:	.ascii	"Please enter text message: "	
61.	.end		

Listing 7.7: Block transfer instruction copies multiple registers

Go ahead and assemble, link, and execute the program as shown in Listing 7.11. Notice the asterisk in the display when a short line like "Test" is input. Where did they come from? Why is everything on one line rather than on separate lines? Here's a clue: The character code for the asterisk is 0x2A and that of the line feed character (resulting from the Enter key), has a code of 0x0A.

```
~$ as -o vector.o vector.s
~$ ld -o vector vector.o
~$ ./vector
Please enter text message:
ABCdefGhIjKlMnOpQrStUvWXYZ
ABCdefGhIjKlMnOpQrStUvWXYZ
abcDEFgHiJkLmNoPQrStUvWXYZ
abcdefghijklmnopQrStUvWXYZ
Please enter text message: Test
Test
tEST*test*Please enter text message: Good Day!
Good Day!
gOODdAY*good day!*Please enter text message:

~$
```

Listing 7.8: Changing the case of the first 16 letters

— 8 —
NEON

One way to improve performance is to perform multiple operations in parallel. The NEON coprocessor provides SIMD (Single Instruction Multiple Data) capability where the same instruction, such as multiplication, is performed on multiple pairs of numbers "at the same time."

The NEON coprocessor is an independent processor having its own set of registers and instructions. It does not contain its own memory for program and data storage, but "watches" all the instructions that the ARM processor is fetching. Basically, a SIMD operation is performed by the following programming sequence:

1. One or more coprocessor instructions move source data into the desired NEON registers.
2. Perform the desired SIMD operation using a NEON coprocessor "vector" instruction (i.e., VADD, VORR, VEOR, ...).
3. Use another NEON instruction to move the result into either one of the ARM's registers or memory.

The NEON coprocessor contains a 2048-bit register file along with logical, integer, and floating point operations. How are these 2048 bits grouped? As registers, they are grouped as 16 128-bit Quad registers, 32 64-bit Double registers, and 32 32-bit Single registers. All three of these register types share the same physical bits. Figure 8.1 shows the correspondence of the first two Q registers with the D and S registers.

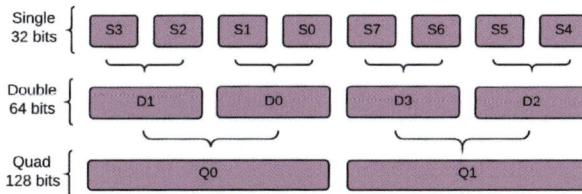

Figure 8.1: Overlap of NEON registers: Bits 0 of S3, 0 of D1, and 0 of Q0 are the same physical bit.

In Chapter 7, we examined bit-by-bit logical operations using the inclusive OR and the exclusive OR, which worked on 32 bits simultaneously. NEON supports bit-by-bit logical operations on either 64 or 128 bits at a time. The vector program from Listing 7.10 will now be slightly modified to use NEON vector instructions to load, store, and perform logical operations on 128 bits.

The modification begins with line 29. Although I have left in most of the previous instructions that performed the logical operations, they have no effect because I have have "commented them out" by putting an @ in the first column. This way, you can see which ARM instructions have been replaced by NEON instructions.

1.	.global	_start	@ Program starting address for linker
2.			
3. @	Display prompt message		
4.			
5. _start:	ldr	R1,=prompt	@ Load pointer to message.
6.	mov	R2,#27	@ Number of characters in message
7.	mov	R0,#1	@ Stdout: Standard output (usually monitor)
8.	mov	R7,#4	@ Linux command code to write
9.	svc	0	@ Call Linux command.
10.			
11. @	Read input line from user keyboard or redirected file.		
12.			
13.	ldr	R1,=msg	@ Memory address to receive input
14.	mov	R0,#0	@ Stdin: Standard input (usually keyboard)
15.	mov	R7,#3	@ Linux command code to read
16.	mov	R2,#30	@ Maximum length to receive
17.	svc	0	@ Issue command to read.
18.			
19. @	Echo line just input back to the user.		
20.			
21.	mov	R2,R0	@ Number of characters input
22.	mov	R0,#1	@ Code for stdout (usually the monitor)
23.	mov	R7,#4	@ Linux service command code to write
24.	svc	0	@ Call Linux command.
25.			
26. @	Change case of first 16 lettters and echo again		
27.			
28.	ldr	R6,=cvt	@ Load pointer to 0x20202020
29. @	ldr	R12,[R6]	@ Load 32-bit pattern into R12
30.	vldm	R6,{Q1}	@ Load 128 bit conversion pattern.
31. @	ldmia	R1,{R8-R11}	@ Load first 16 characters input
32.	vldm	R1,{Q0}	@ Load first 16 characters input
33. @	eor	R8,R8,R12	@ "Flip" the case of 4 letters.
34. @	eor	R9,R9,R12	@ "Flip" the case of 4 letters.
35. @	eor	R10,R10,R12	@ "Flip" the case of 4 letters.
36. @	eor	R11,R11,R12	@ "Flip" the case of 4 letters.
37.	veor	Q0,Q0,Q1	@ Flip case on 16 letters.
38. @	stmia	R1,{R8-R11}	@ Overlay with changed case letters.
39.	vstm	R1,{Q0}	@ Overlay 16 changed case letters.
40.	mov	R0,#1	@ [R0] = stdout (R1, R2, R7 still OK)
41.	svc	0	@ Call Linux command to display again.

```
42.
43. @          Convert to lower case and echo again
44.
45.    vorr    Q0,Q0,Q1      @ Convert 16 letters to lower case.
46.    vstm    R1,{Q0}       @ Overlay with lower case letters.
47.    mov     R0,#1         @ [R0] = stdout (R1, R2, R7 still OK)
48.    svc     0             @ Call Linux command to display again.
49.
50. @          Go get another line, but exit if only "Enter" key input.
51.
52.    cmp     R2,#1         @ Test if only the line feed character.
53.    bgt     _start        @ Loop back around to get another input.
54.    mov     R7,#1         @ Command 1 terminates programs.
55.    mov     R0,#0         @ Set exit code to zero.
56.    svc     0             @ Return full control to Linux.
57.
58.    .data
59. cvt:   .word   0x20202020,0x20202020,0x20202020,0x20202020
60. msg:   .ds     15        @ Memory buffer for keyboard input
61. prompt: .ascii  "Please enter text message: "
62.    .end
```

Listing 8.1: Changing case of 16 letters using NEON instructions.

The following new lines of code in Listing 8.1 are of particular interest:

- 30: Vector Load Multiple (VLDM) copies 16 byte pattern into 128-bit NEON Q1 register. This pattern is in ARM memory at location pointed to by ARM register R6 and contains 16 bytes of x020 (bit 5 is set in each byte).
- 32: Another VLDM loads NEON register Q1 with the first 16 bytes from the message buffer. It replaces the ARM instruction LDMIA which loaded the same 16 bytes into four ARM registers.
- 37: The Vector Exclusive OR (VEOR) instruction operates on 128 bits simultaneously, thereby replacing 4 ARM EOR instructions.
- 39: The Vector Store Multiple VSTM instruction is similar to and thereby replaces the ARM STMIA instruction, but uses a list of NEON data registers. ARM register R1 points to the ARM memory where the NEON data is to be stored.
- 45: The Vector inclusive OR (VORR) instruction operates on 128 bits simultaneously, thereby replacing four ARM ORR instructions. I didn't include the four ORR instructions that are commented out in order to reduce some of the clutter.
- 59: Since all 128 bits will be operated on simultaneously, I needed to expand the conversion pattern to 4 words (16 bytes altogether).

Listing 8.2 shows the assembly, link, and execution using the same sample input data as before. This is identical to Listing 7.11 except the "-mfpu=neon" option is needed on the assembly command to recognize the NEON instructions.

```
~$ as -o vector.o vector.s -mfpu=neon
~$ ld -o vector vector.o
~$ ./vector
Please enter text message: ABCdefGhIjKlMnOpQrStUvWXYZ
ABCdefGhIjKlMnOpQrStUvWXYZ
abcDEFgHiJkLmNoPQrStUvWXYZ
abcdefghijklmnopQrStUvWXYZ
Please enter text message:

~$
```

Listing 8.2: Modify the case of the first 16 letters on the text line.

Scalars and Vectors

A scalar value consists of a single number, and a vector value consists of a group of numbers. Examples of vectors are the position and velocity of an object in a three-dimensional coordinate system which would have X, Y, and Z components, for example. An example of a scalar is the mass of an object (i.e., one number).

Why all the bother? Are vectors used that extensively that it's worth adding confusion to push for a performance gain? Consider the following:

1. In physics and engineering, quantities like position, velocity, and acceleration are all vectors that are measurable quantities.
2. Many scientific and engineering problems are solved using matrix transformations and inversions which require many vector-type multiplications and additions.
3. Graphics applications which display the 3-D world mapped onto a 2-D screen require many matrix multiplications which are efficiently processed by vector instructions.
4. Digital signal processing and many analog to digital conversions work efficiently extensive vector processing.

Lanes

NEON also provides integer arithmetic operations. How do the results from an arithmetic operation such as addition or multiplication compare to one of the logical operations? Logical operations are bit-by-bit, and the results stay in each bit "column," but arithmetic operations must expand to use more bits. Even an example such as $1_2+1_2=10_2$ shows addition can have a carry that requires another bit column. In order to provide multiple simultaneous parallel arithmetic operations, the NEON coprocessor forces arithmetic operations to stay in fixed-sized "lanes" and does not allow the results from one lane to carry (or overflow) into the next.

NEON arithmetic assembly language operations are of the form "Operation.TypeLanesize," such as VADD.U16 and VSUB.S8. NEON arithmetic lane type and size combinations are specified by the type and size suffix:

- S8, S16, S32, S64: Signed integer: High order bit is the sign bit.
- U8, U16, U32, U64: Unsigned integer: High order bit is a data bit.
- I8, I16, I32, I64 : Integer, either signed or unsigned
- F32: Floating point, single precision

In a NEON arithmetic operation, the total number of bits involved is specified by whether a D (64 bits) or a Q (128 bits) register is used. The number of parallel lanes is therefore either 128 or 64 divided by one of the above lane sizes. For example, "VADD.U16   D0,D1" has four lanes (64/16). Although there can be 128 simultaneous 1-bit logical operations performed, the number of simultaneous arithmetic operations is reduced to the number of lanes.

The maximum number of lanes is sixteen (128-bit Q register divided by an 8-bit lane width). Of course, the minimum number of lanes is one, where a 64-bit D register is divided by a 64-bit lane width. As an example of simultaneous computation, the program in Listing 8.3 adds eight 8-bit integers.

The vector program in Listing 8.3 demonstrates eight additions taking places simultaneously in eight 8-bit lanes. It's output demonstrates the results of staying in each lane without overflowing into the next.

1. Macro dispbs will be called to display the contents of a byte in decimal. It is identical to that already used in Chapter 6.
2. Outer loop: Add the contents of each lane to themselves, and display the eight totals on the display screen.
3. Inner loop: Eight lanes are being used. Although the NEON instruction adds all eight lanes simultaneously, the display routine will have to loop through the eight values to display them.

Take note of the following lines in Listing 8.3:

- 18: Outer loop is initialized for four passes through the loop.
- 24: Top of inner loop which displays the contents of the eight lanes.
- 27: Macro dispbs outputs one of the lanes in decimal. Note: Change the 10 to a 2 to display the lane in binary if you like.
- 32: NEON instruction VADD.U8 adds eight lanes of data. Each time this instruction executes the data is doubled.
- 36: Bottom of outer loop.
- 43: List of eight numbers. Note: The last few are large enough to force an overflow condition when the program is run

```
1.     .global    _start         @ Program starting address for linker
2.
3. @          Macro "dispbs base,tail" calls v_dig1, then displays a character.
4. @                    base:   Base (2 - 16) in which to display number
5. @                    tail:   Separation character to be output
6.
7.     .macro     dispbs   base, tail
8.     push       {R0,R1}        @ Save values from R0 and R1.
9.     mov        R0,#\base      @ Load base for display.
10.    bl         v_dig1         @ Display number in base ...
11.    ldr        R1,=\tail      @ Separation character.
12.    bl         v_asc1         @ Display single character.
13.    pop        {R0,R1}        @ Restore original values.
14.    .endm
15.
16. @          Initialize 64-bit NEON register D1 with eight 8-bit integers and R5.
17.
18. _start:    mov        R5,#4          @ Number of loops of eight 8-bit additions.
19.            ldr        R1,=intlst     @ Pointer to list of integers.
20.            vldm       R1,{D1}        @ Load eight 8-bit integers into D1.
21.
22. @          Loop to display array of eight 8-bit numbers in decimal.
23.
24. addlp:     ldr        R1,=sumlst     @ Pointer to first 8-bit number.
25.            vstm       R1,{D1}        @ Store 64 bits in 8 bytes.
26.            mov        R6,#7          @ Number of elements in array - 1
27. dloop:     dispbs     10,tab         @ Display next byte in decimal.
28.            add        R1,#1          @ Point to next byte to display.
29.            subs       R6,#1          @ Number of bytes remaining.
30.            bgt        dloop          @ Continue loop until message complete.
31.            dispbs     10,newln       @ Display last byte in decimal.
32.            vadd.u8    D1,D1,D1       @ Double each 8-bit integer in D1.
33.
34. @          Continue the loop until all passes done.
```

```
35.
36.            subs      R5,#1        @ Decrement number of passes remaining.
37.            bgt       addlp        @ Go perform another pass through loop.
38.            mov       R7,#1        @ Command 1 terminates programs.
39.            mov       R0,#0        @ Set exit code to zero.
40.            svc       0            @ Return full control to Linux.
41.
42.            .data
43. intlst:    .byte     1,2,10,50,100,150,200,250
44. sumlst:    .ds       4            @ Reserve 8 bytes of memory,
45. newln:     .ascii    "\n"         @ Line feed character code
46. tab:       .ascii    "\t"         @ Horizontal tab character code
47.            .end
```

Listing 8.3: NEON coprocessor performing eight 8-bit additions simultaneously

Assemble, link, and execute the new version of the vector program using the previous set of commands (shown in Listing 8.2). The output from running the program is provided in Listing 8.4.

1	2	10	50	100	150	200	250
2	4	20	100	200	44	144	244
4	8	40	200	144	88	32	232
8	16	80	144	32	176	64	208

Listing 8.4: Adding eight lanes (i.e., columns) simultaneously

The first three lanes (i.e., columns in the display) look fine, For example in lane 1: $1 + 1 = 2$, $2 + 2 = 4$, and $4 + 4 = 8$. However, in lane 4 where $50 + 50 = 100$ and $100 + 100 = 200$ is correct, a problem appears with $200 + 200 = 144$. Overflow has occurred! The sum $200 + 200 = 400$, which will not fit in an 8-bit lane. The maximum unsigned value that can fit in 8 bits is 255. The other incorrect values in the output shown in Listing 8.4 have similar overflow problems.

What would be the results if we used VADD.S8 on line 32 so that we would be working with 8-bit signed integers? The output display would actually be the same. All of the results will be the same whether you used an I8, S8, or U8 suffix, and this would also be true of 16-bit, 32-bit, and 64-bit lanes. So are these three suffixes synonymous, and is there nothing that can be done about overflow conditions giving ridiculous looking results? The answer to both of these questions is no. NEON provides two features to alleviate or at least soften the overflow problem: Saturation (Q) and Wide (W) lanes.

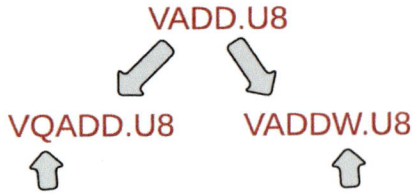

Figure 8.2: NEON Saturation and Wide Lanes

Saturation Integer Arithmetic

By using VQADD instead of VADD, the NEON coprocessor still can't provide the correct answer in the case of an overflow, but it will keep the answer as close as possible. Figure 8.3 repeats the results of Listing 8.4 detailing the three lanes that overflowed on the first pass through the loop.

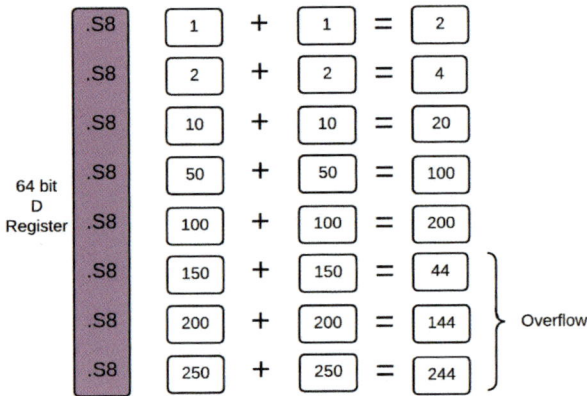

Figure 8.3 Eight lanes added in parallel with three resulting in overflows

Let's continue with the same test program and change the VADD on line 32 to VQADD. Recompile, link, and execute the program and watch the sums march to their saturation limits in Listing 8.5.

1	2	10	50	100	150	200	250
2	4	20	100	200	255	255	255
4	8	40	200	255	255	255	255
8	16	80	255	255	255	255	255

Listing 8.5: Output with VQADD.U8 instead of VADD.U8

Assembly Language Coding in Color

For signed S8 operations, the extreme limits for an 8-bit signed integer are -128 and 127. For unsigned U8 operations, the limits are 0 and 255. What are the limits for the generalized integer code of I8? Since the limits aren't specified in I8, NEON cannot know the limits. Therefore, the I8, I16, I32, and I64 suffixes are not allowed to be used with the Q saturation modification.

Figure 8.4 illustrates the comparison of unsigned saturated integer addition to unsaturated addition. If 16-bit lanes are used with VQADD or any of the other saturated arithmetic operations, the range for unsigned numbers would be 0 through 65,635. Signed saturation examples can easily be done by using the S8 suffix on line 32 of the program. The data input on line 43 can be either positive or negative, but should fall within the range of -128 through +127. The v_dig1 subroutine will also be modified to test for bit 7 being set indicating a negative number (see Appendix B).

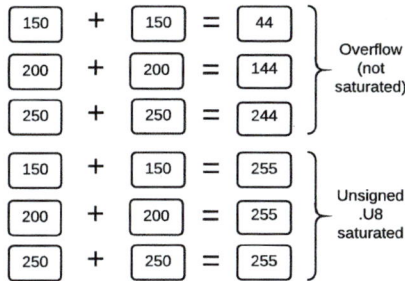

Figure 8.4: Effect of using unsigned saturation addition

Promotions to Wide Lanes

Although addition of two large binary numbers can overflow by a single bit and be lost, it is not unusual for the product of two very large numbers to require double the number of bits of the factors. Most CPUs have a special "long" multiply instruction to accommodate this situation. In the ARM, the UMULL instruction multiplies two 32-bit integers that produces a 64-bit product that is then stored in two registers. NEON, however, takes this a step further and provides "long" modifications for most of its instructions. As an example, the VADD instruction has the following modifications:

- VADDL: Long: The result is placed in a lane that is twice the size of operands.
- VADDN: Narrow: The result is placed in a lane that is half the size of operands.
- VADDW: Wide: The result is the same size as that of the first operand, but the second operand is half the size of the first.

Interleaved Load and Store

Using parallel computation, the NEON processor can substantially improve total throughput in processing data stored in tables and arrays. However, setting up the proper combinations of operands and loading them into the right sets of registers may be awkward and inefficient in itself. NEON has interleaved load and store instructions to meet this challenge of array data which is stored in various patterns in memory. They can transfer up to four quad words (512 bits) at a time between the NEON's registers and the ARM's memory.

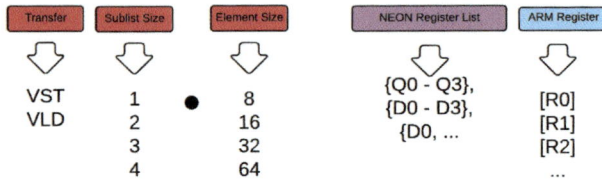

Transfer	Sublist Size	Element Size	NEON Register List	ARM Register
⇩	⇩	⇩	⇩	⇩
VST	1	● 8	{Q0 - Q3},	[R0]
VLD	2	16	{D0 - D3},	[R1]
	3	32	{D0, ...	[R2]
	4	64		...

Figure 8.5: Interleaved store and load instructions

Figure 8.5 summarizes the interleaved store and load instructions that are available with NEON.

- As few as one 64-bit D register and as many as 4 adjacent 128-bit Q registers are processed with one instruction (minimum of 64 bits and maximum of 512 bits).
- A memory array is composed of multiple elements of the same size which can be 8, 16, 32, or 64 bits in length.
- Elements are moved sequentially between ARM memory and one or more NEON registers.
- An ARM R register acts as an index and contains the byte address of the next element to load/store in the ARM's memory.
- The ARM index register may be updated if the write-back bit is set ([R4]!, for example).

A new program appears in Listing 8.6 to demonstrate some of the possible storage patterns available with the VST (vector store) instruction. A test pattern of 24 characters, A through X, is loaded into registers D0, D1, and D2, and the following four instructions will demonstrate how NEON interleaved instructions work:

- VST1.8   {D0-D2},[R1]
- VST3.8   {D0-D2},[R1]
- VST3.16   {D0-D2},[R1]
- VST3.32   {D0-D2},[R1]

Take note of the following critical lines in this program:.

- 3: Initialize registers D0, D1, and D2 with test pattern (A through X).
- 5: Write the test pattern back into memory in its original order.
- 9: First display line is the original order of 24 characters.
- 13, 16, 19, 22: VST1.8, VST3.8, VST3.16, VST3.32,

1.	.global	_start	@ Starting address for linker
2. _start:	ldr	R1,=A2X	@ Memory buffer for output from NEON.
3.	vldm	R1,{D0-D2}	@ Load "AB...WX" into 3 64-bit registers.
4.	ldr	R1,=result	@ Memory buffer for "interleaved" output.
5.	vstm	R1,{D0-D2}	@ Save exact copy for display.
6.	mov	R2,#25	@ Length of buffer including line feed
7.	mov	R0,#1	@ Stdout: Standard output (monitor)
8.	mov	R7,#4	@ Linux command code to write
9.	svc	0	@ Display exact copy from VLDM/VSTM.
10.			
11. @		Show interleaved store using vst1.8, vst3.8, vst3.16, and vst3.32	
12.			
13.	vst1.8	{D0–D2},[R1]	@ Save as 1 "element" of 8 bits each
14.	mov	R0,#1	@ Reset to Stdout: (changed by SVC call)
15.	svc	0	@ Display exact copy from VLDM/VSTM.
16.	vst3.8	{D0–D2},[R1]	@ Save as 3 "elements" of 8 bits each
17.	mov	R0,#1	@ Reset to Stdout: (changed by SVC call)
18.	svc	0	@ Display exact copy from VLDM/VSTM.
19.	vst3.16	{D0–D2},[R1]	@ Save as 3 "elements" of 16 bits each
20.	mov	R0,#1	@ Reset to Stdout: (changed by SVC call)
21.	svc	0	@ Display exact copy from VLDM/VSTM.
22.	vst3.32	{D0–D2},[R1]	@ Save as 3 "elements" of 32 bits each
23.	mov	R0,#1	@ Reset to Stdout: (changed by SVC call)
24.	svc	0	@ Display exact copy from VLDM/VSTM.
25.			
26.	mov	R0,#0	@ Status 0 indicates "normal completion"
27.	mov	R7,#1	@ Service command terminates this program.
28.	svc	0	@ Issue Linux command to stop program.
29.	.data		
30. A2X:	.ascii	"ABCDEFGHIJKLMNOPQRSTUVWX" @ 24 bytes	
31. result:	.ds	12	@ Reserve room for "interleaved" store.
32.	.ascii	"\n"	@ Line feed
33.	.end		

Listing 8.6: NEON interleaved storage example

Listing 8.7 displays the output from running this program. The first line simply stores the register data back into memory using the STM store multiple instruction on line 6. The remaining display lines result from four interleaved storage instructions on lines 13, 16, 19, and 22, which will be explained in the following paragraphs.

```
ABCDEFGHIJKLMNOPQRSTUVWX
ABCDEFGHIJKLMNOPQRSTUVWX
AIQBJRCKSDLTEMUFNVGOWHPX
ABIJQRCDKLSTEFMNUVGHOPWX
ABCDIJKLQRSTEFGHMNOPUVWX
```

Listing 8.7: Output from interleaved storage example program

The first two lines of the output seem reasonable to everyone, but some people might be surprised that the test pattern loaded into the NEON registers is the following:

- D0: "HGFEDCBA"
- D1: "PONMLKJI"
- D2: "XWVUTSRQ"

Does this seem to be backwards? It's what is known as "little endian" format. As seen in Figure 8.6, the first byte from the memory buffer is loaded first into the "little end" (i.e., bit 0) of the register, and the following bytes keep moving in until the "big end" is reached.

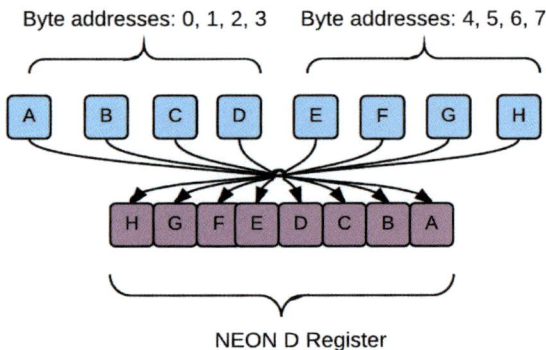

Figure 8.6: NEON loads data into registers in little endian format

Assembly Language Coding in Color

Actually, the same is true for loading ARM registers from memory, but the ARM has a status bit that can be set to enable "big endian" format, where the first byte from memory is loaded into the "big end" of a register.

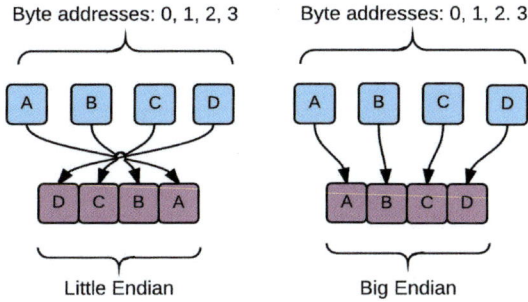

Figure 8.7: ARM supports both little and big endian formats

Interleaved storage instructions are analogous to eating dinner. I will eat all the carrots, beans, and fish on my plate, but in what order should I eat them? Do I eat all the carrots before moving on to eat all the beans, and then all the fish, or do I mix them together by taking a bite of carrots, then a bite of beans, then a bite of fish, and back to the carrots until everything is gone?

The VST1.8 on line 13 is like eating all my carrots before starting on my beans. The "1" in VST1 indicates I want all the bits transferred from one register before moving onto the next. The "8" is the element size which is analogous to the size of a mouthful, and here indicates that VST1 will be transferring 8 bits at a time. As you might suspect, the VST1.8 storage pattern will look identical to that from VSTM.

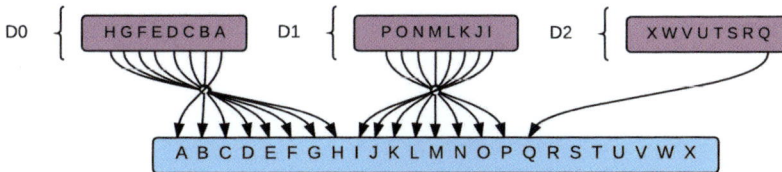

Figure 8.8: VST1.8 {D0-D2},[R1]

Output Line	Instruction
ABCDEFGHIJKLMNOPQRSTUVWX	VSTM R1,{D0-D2}
ABCDEFGHIJKLMNOPQRSTUVWX	VST1.8 {D0-D2},[R1]
AIQBJRCKSDLTEMUFNVGOWHPX	VST3.8 {D0-D2},[R1]
ABIJQRCDKLSTEFMNUVGHOPWX	VST3.16 {D0-D2},[R1]
ABCDIJKLQRSTEFGHMNOPUVWX	VST3.32 {D0-D2},[R1]

Table 8.1: Output and the instructions that generated each line

On line 16 of the program, the VST3.8 instruction says I will still be moving data in groups of 8-bits (the element size), but I will be taking them from a subset of three adjacent registers. This is analogous to eating a bite of carrots, then a bite of beans, and finally a bite of fish, before going back to get the next round of carrots, beans, and fish, etc.

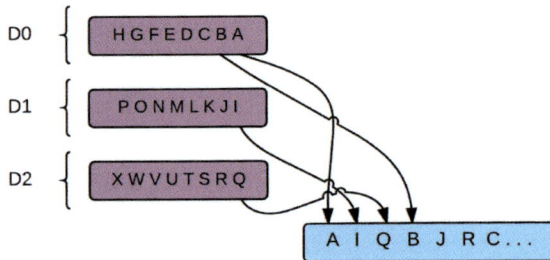

Figure 8.9: VST3.8 {D0-D2},[R1]

Figure 8.10 is the same as 8.9 except I'm taking bigger "mouthfuls": 16 bits instead of 8. The VST3.16 on line 19 says I will be moving data in as 16-bit elements, and I will be taking them from a subset of three adjacent registers.

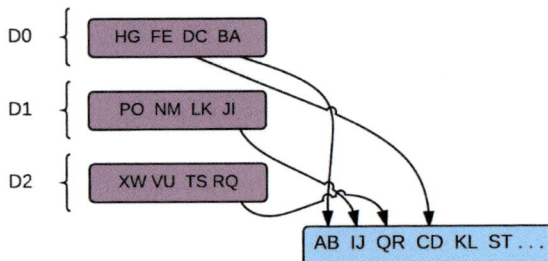

Figure 8.10: VST3.16 {D0-D2},[R1]

Assembly Language Coding in Color

Figure 8.11 again uses 3 registers, but now 32 bits are moved at a time.

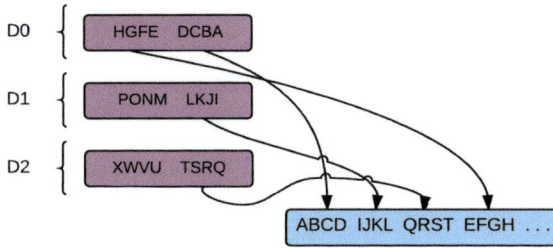

Figure 8.11: VST3.32 {D0-D2},[R1]

Can I use a VST2 instruction? Yes, but not with three registers in the list. My list would have to be either {D0,D1} or {D0-D3}. "Left overs" are not allowed. The number of registers in the list can be between one and four, but must be a multiple of the sublist size specified adjacent to the "VST."

Floating Point

The main theme associated with the NEON coprocessor is the simultaneous execution of multple sets of numbers associated with a single instruction. I have only demonstrated a few of the instructions that are available, but I do want to whet your appetite for further study. For instance, the NEON coprocessor provides excellent support for floating point numbers used in engineering and scientific applications. As you can see from Figure 8.12, even representing a number such as decimal 13 is somewhat more complicated than what we have been working with thus far. However, you should now have adaquate background to dig deeper.

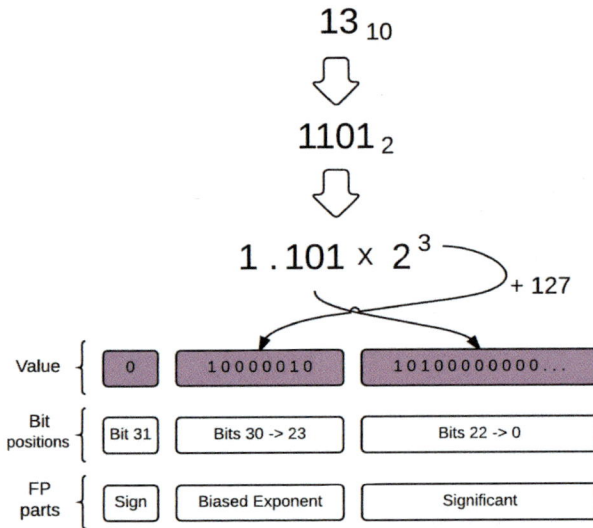

$$13_{10}$$

$$\Downarrow$$

$$1101_2$$

$$\Downarrow$$

$$1.101 \times 2^3$$

$$+ 127$$

Value	0	10000010	10100000000...

Bit positions	Bit 31	Bits 30 -> 23	Bits 22 -> 0

FP parts	Sign	Biased Exponent	Significant

Figure 8.12: Single precision floating point fields in IEEE 754 format

Conclusion

Aristotle is credited with the saying, "The more you know, the more you know you don't know." I look at learning assembly language not so much as a target, but as a springboard. While closing a few loose ends in this conclusion, I will open up a few new topics you may want to pursue. The goal of this book is to assist students and computer enthusiasts to get on a solid path to understanding computer architecture.

Technical Reference Manual: The focus of this book is to get students programming and understanding the architecture as quickly as possible using the most common instructions. You should now be at a comfortable point to understand the details covered in ARM and NEON technical specification documents. Note: There are several versions of the ARM processor. I've basically been describing the Cortex-A7 and Cortex-A8 versions.

Debugger: A very informative tool for observing what is happening within an assembly language program is a debugger. The GNU gdb debugger program is present on almost all Linux distributions. By setting of breakpoints or single stepping through a program, the memory contents, register contents, and flags can be observed.

Interrupt Processing: In a real-time embedded systems program, there are basically two approaches that can be used to determine when a device requires attention from the software: polling and interrupts. In the polling approach, the software must loop though all possible devices, reading the status of each and deciding what to do with any status changes. This approach is very controlled and relatively easy to implement. The problem is it wastes a lot of time checking devices that do not need attention while devices that do need immediate attention have to wait their turn.

In the interrupt approach, the I/O hardware essentially "calls" a device driver (similar to a subroutine) using an "instruction" that behaves almost identical to the SVC instruction we've been using.

Supervisor Mode: The ARM processor design enables multiprogramming where multiple users can be sharing the same CPU and memory at virtually the same time. One responsibility of an operating system, such as Linux, is to protect one user from another while they are in the same memory space and taking turns using the CPU. This capability requires the operating system to run in a privileged, or supervisory, state where it can have access to all of memory, while user programs are restricted to their own data areas.

The ARM processor has four modes in which it can operate. In this book, we've operated entirely in the user mode, where we are restricted from using a few powerful instructions. The other three modes are in supervisory mode.

Floating Point: Floating point format is a container for real numbers, like those from measurements and those required in scientific notation such as 6.02×10^{23}.

Individuals interested in more depth and covering subjects like floating point, software development, and the use of the debugger should consider my other book: *Assembly Language Using the Raspberry Pi: A Hardware Software Bridge*.

Appendix A
Raspberry Pi Setup

Most readers of this book will have their Raspberry Pi computers already working. For those of you who do not, I've included this brief appendix. If you're totally new to computers and the Raspberry Pi, then you will want to follow more detailed setup instructions from the Internet or another book.

This appendix also includes Linux configuration parameters related to assembly language programming and download instruction for obtaining the source code for the assembly language programs developed in this book.

GNU Assembler

This book is a tutorial for learning assembly language using the Raspberry Pi or similar computer. The information presented and examples given are specifically for the Raspberry Pi 2 and 3, but should also work fine for previous and future versions with the possible exception for the examples using the NEON coprocessor.

The main constituent of the Raspberry Pi is the ARM CPU, so this book uses the GNU assembler from the Free Software Foundation that is included with the Raspian Linux kernel distribution for the Raspberry Pi. This software is not part of the Raspberry Pi itself, but is included with almost all packages sold that include the Raspberry Pi circuit board, power supply, case, and SD memory card. If the Raspian Linux distribution software is not included with the NOOBS (New Out Of the Box Software) present on the SD card, it may be downloaded over the Internet for free from various Internet sites.

The Hash Symbol (#)

The GNU "as" assembler program uses the hash symbol (#) to identify immediate constants. If the British currency symbol appears instead of the hash, it is probably due to the keyboard not being configured correctly. For users in the United States, this configuration is normally adjusted by entering the following from the Linux command line and selecting the US Keyboard option as follows.

sudo raspi-config

Language English US Keyboard(9) US

Source Code

This book contains over 20 program listings as examples of ARM and NEON coding. I have made them available on the Internet so they can be easily downloaded using the git utility and GitHub website. GitHub "is a code hosting platform for version control and collaboration." It is composed of multiple public and private "repositories" holding text, image, and video files. Enter the following command from the Linux command prompt to create directory *RPi_Asm_Bridge* and load all the program listings for this book into it.

git clone https://github.com/robertdunne/RPi_Asm_Color.git

Of course, you must already have your Raspberry Pi configured for Internet access. In the event the git utility is not already present on your system, it can be downloaded and installed using the following command line:

sudo apt install git

Once you have the program listings, please display details related to their use from the README file by entering the following command or use any text editor of your choosing.

cat README.md

Warning: The assembler source code that appears in this book and is available for download is for learning to program in assembly language. Some of these subroutines are incomplete and even contain problems that are used as examples. No guarantee of their commercial utility is expressed or implied.

Alternatives to the I/O formatting subroutines presented in this book are contained in the CLIB library, but there are conditions and restrictions for their use in commercial applications as well.

BeagleBone Black

Although this book was designed for use with the Raspberry Pi, other Linux-based systems having an ARM CPU, NEON coprocessor, and GNU utilities will also work fine. For the BeagleBone Black, I recommend running Linux command mode using the PuTTY program. The IP address of the BeagleBone Black attached to a PC through the USB cable is (192.168.7.2).

Appendix B
Binary Numbers

To be precise, it's not the numbers that are binary, but the written representation of numbers. For example, we currently count eight planets in the solar system. This has been "written down" as 8, VIII, 10_8, 1000_2, as well as a variety of other representations throughout history.

What's Binary?

Binary means *two* like a binary star system consisting of a pair of stars. In the case of binary "numbers," the *two* refers to the base, also known as the radix, which indicates how many different symbols (or digits) can be used. In our every day decimal (base 10) system, there are ten symbols available {0, 1, 2, 3, 4, 5, 6, 7, 8, 9} so we can represent a number in a form like 3274, 1620, and 36. While in binary (base 2), we have only two symbols available {0, 1} so we are restricted to representing numbers in a form like 1100, 10101, 1, and 111. Other popular bases that have been used in the computer industry are octal (base 8) having eight symbols {0, 1, 2, 3, 4, 5, 6, 7} and hexadecimal (base 16) having sixteen symbols {0, 1, 2, 3, 4, 5, 6, 7, 8, 9, A, B, C, D, E, F}.

Why Binary?

The simple answer is that the logical building blocks (i.e., electronics in today's systems) are simpler and more efficient in binary than they are in our everyday decimal. The electronic logic circuits have two states: High and Low (voltage levels) which can model a variety of binary states like True and False, Yes and No, and of course One and Zero. This system follows the logic attributed to Aristotle thousands of years ago.

In the following table, we compare the written representations of counting from 0 to 12 in five different bases. Notice how the rightmost column (one's place) is incremented through all of the possible symbols available in the base before the next column to its left is incremented.

base 10 10 symbols {0123456789}	base 2 2 symbols {01}	base 3 3 symbols {012}	base 4 4 symbols {0123}	base 5 5 symbols {01234}
0	0	0	0	0
1	1	1	1	1
2	10	2	2	2
3	11	10	3	3
4	100	11	10	4
5	101	12	11	10
6	110	20	12	11
7	111	21	13	12
8	1000	22	20	13
9	1001	100	21	14
10	1010	101	22	20
11	1011	102	23	21
12	1100	110	30	22

Table B.1: Counting from 0 to 12 in bases 10, 2, 3, 4, and 5

Column	3	2	1	0
Base 10	$10^3=1000$	$10^2=100$	$10^1=10$	$10^0=1$
Base 2	$2^3=8$	$2^2=4$	$2^1=2$	$2^0=1$
Base 3	$3^3=27$	$3^2=9$	$3^1=3$	$3^0=1$
Base 4	$4^3=64$	$4^2=16$	$4^1=4$	$4^0=1$
Base 5	$5^3=125$	$5^2=25$	$5^1=5$	$5^0=1$

Table B.2: Value of each column in bases 10, 2, 3, 4, and 5

The Problems with Binary

The problems with binary are not with computers, but with us humans:

1. We are comfortable with base ten and have used it daily for most of our lives.
2. Binary numbers are awkward for us due to the large number of columns required. Who would prefer replacing the decimal representation of 7094, 1620, 1108, 6600, 3033, and 7800 with their binary equivalents 1101110110110, 11001010100, 10001010100, 1100111001000, 101111011001, and 1111001111000?

Assembly Language Coding in Color

3. Conversion between binary and decimal is difficult to do "in our heads." The difficulty stems from the fact that 10 is not an integer power of two.

Superscripts and Subscripts

In math books, the base (or radix) used to represent a number is given as a subscript. For example: a number written in decimal would be like 257_{10} and in binary it would be like 10000001_2. If no subscript is provided, we assume it is decimal unless it is stated in the text that the numbers are expressed in a different base such as binary. When working with computer programs, whether assembler or higher level, subscripts are not commonly available so binary is generally entered as 0b10101, 10101b, or %10101 depending on the computer system or application being used.

Superscripts indicate a number raised to a power. For example, 4^3 means $4\times4\times4$ equaling 64 and 2^8 is $2\times2\times2\times2\times2\times2\times2\times2$ equaling 256. Also recall that 2^0, 10^0, 16^0, and any non-zero number raised to the zeroth power equals one.

A decimal number is really a short notation for a polynomial of powers of 10. For example: 137_{10} is $1\times10^2 + 3\times10^1 + 7\times10^0$ which is $100 + 30 + 7$. Likewise, a binary number is really a short notation for a polynomial of powers of 2. For example: 110101_2 is $1\times2^5 + 1\times2^4 + 0\times2^3 + 1\times2^2 + 0\times2^1 + 1\times2^0$. By the way, this polynomial structure is the main reason we label and count bits within a byte or word from right to left starting with zero.

Bit Position	3	2	1	0
Power of 2	$2^3=8$	$2^2=4$	$2^1=2$	$2^0=1$
Binary example	1	0	1	1
$1011_2 = 1 \times 2^3 + 0 \times 2^2 + 1 \times 2^1 + 1 \times 2^0 = 8 + 0 + 2 + 1 = 11_{10}$				

Table B.3: Bit position example: $1011_2 = 2^3 + 0 + 2^1 + 2^0 = 8 + 0 + 2 + 1 = 11_{10}$

Conversion to Any Base

A popular way to convert a number to a particular base is successive division. The remainders from each division will provide the digits (i.e., symbols) beginning with rightmost digit. For example, converting the number 3274 to decimal follows:

1. $3274 / 10 = 327$ Remainder 4

2. $327 / 10 = 32$ Remainder 7
3. $32 / 10 = 3$ Remainder 2
4. $3 / 10 = 0$ Remainder 3

So the "number" 3274 is represented in decimal as the sequence of remainders "3" "2" "7" and "4." By the way: This technique of successively dividing a number by the desired base works regardless of how the "computer" internally stores numbers. It could be binary, decimal, or any conceivable internal structure that would permit division.

Converting the same number 3274 to binary follows:

1. $3274 / 2 = 1637$ Remainder 0
2. $1637 / 2 = 818$ Remainder 1
3. $818 / 2 = 409$ Remainder 0
4. $409 / 2 = 204$ Remainder 1
5. $204 / 2 = 102$ Remainder 0
6. $102 / 2 = 51$ Remainder 0
7. $51 / 2 = 25$ Remainder 1
8. $25 / 2 = 12$ Remainder 1
9. $12 / 2 = 6$ Remainder 0
10. $6 / 2 = 3$ Remainder 0
11. $3 / 2 = 1$ Remainder 1
12. $1 / 2 = 0$ Remainder 1

So the "number" 3274 is represented in binary as the sequence of remainders "1" "1" "0" "0" "1" "1" "0" "0" "1" "0" "1" and "0." As an exercise, try converting 3274 to base five by successively dividing by five until the quotient is zero ($3274/5 = 654$ remainder 4, ...). The answer will be 101044_5.

Multiplying and Dividing by Shifting

If we want to multiply by ten "in our heads" in our everyday decimal system, we just append a zero. For example to multiply 709 by 10, we append "0" to "709" and get "7090." Likewise, when we multiply by 100 (i.e., 10^2), we append two zeroes, and for 1000, we append 3 zeroes, etc. For dividing by powers of ten, we do the reverse: we remove zeroes on the right. What if there are not enough zeros present on the right? Then we move the decimal point. For example to divide 1108 by 100, we move the decimal point to the left two places giving us 11.08.

When we shift a number to the left in base two, we are multiplying by a power of two, and when we shift to the right, we are dividing by a power of two. This means that conversion into and from binary format is done very efficiently using shifting rather than division. Converting the same number 3274 (110011001010_2) to binary by shifting is below. Note: The notation ">> 1" means shift 1 bit position to the right, and the "Carry out" refers to the rightmost bit that is lost when the value is shifted.

1. 110011001010 >> 1 = 11001100101 with Carry out 0
2. 11001100101 >> 1 = 1100110010 Carry out 1
3. 1100110010 >> 1 = 110011001 Carry out 0
4. 110011001 >> 1 = 11001100 Carry out 1
5. 11001100 >> 1 = 1100110 Carry out 0
6. 1100110 >> 1 = 110011 Carry out 0
7. 110011 >> 1 = 11001 Carry out 1
8. 11001 >> 1 = 1100 Carry out 1
9. 1100 >> 1 = 110 Carry out 0
10. 110 >> 1 = 11 Carry out 0
11. 11 >> 1 = 1 Carry out 1
12. 1 >> 1 = 0 Carry out 1

Converting Digits Into a Number

To convert "written digits" into a number, run the above process in reverse: Do successive multiplications. For example in base 10: the sequence of digits "1" "6" "2" "2" could be used to "build" the number 1622 as follows:

1. Start with 0
2. $0 \times 10 + 1 = 1$
3. $1 \times 10 + 6 = 16$
4. $16 \times 10 + 2 = 162$
5. $162 \times 10 + 2 = 1622$

In binary, it is simply a matter of shifting to the left one bit position to "multiply" by two. In the following example, the number expressed as a sequence of digits "110011001010" is built by a series of logical left shifts notated by "<< 1" combined with a logical OR notated by "+":

1. Start with 0
2. 0 << 1 + 1 = 1
3. 1 << 1 + 1 = 11
4. 11 << 1 + 0 = 110
5. 110 << 1 + 0 = 1100
6. 1100 << 1 + 1 = 11001
7. 11001 << 1 + 1 = 110011
8. 110011 << 1 + 0 = 1100110
9. 1100110 << 1 + 0 = 11001100
10. 11001100 << 1 + 1 = 110011001
11. 110011001 << 1 + 0 = 1100110010
12. 1100110010 << 1 + 1 = 11001100101
13. 11001100101 << 1 + 0 = 110011001010

Negative Binary Numbers

When we include negative numbers, we effectively double how many numbers we have to be able to represent in binary. For every positive number, we have a corresponding negative number. This requires an additional bit, a "sign" bit, that has to be associated with every binary number in registers and storage.

Rather than append an additional bit to each numeric storage type, computer manufacturers have chosen to steal a bit from the positive range. Instead of an 8-bit byte supporting numbers in the range of 0 through 255, it supports -128 through +127 for "signed" bytes. Likewise, signed half-words have a range of -32,768 to +32,767 rather than 0 through 65,535 for the unsigned format. The range is actually the same, but it has been shifted by 50%.

There have been four formats popular for representing signed numbers in binary computers:

- **Bias:** Add ½ the total range to all numbers
- **Sign and magnitude:** High order (leftmost) bit is the sign: 1 for negative
- **One's complement:** Complement (i.e., toggle) all bits for negative.
- **Two's complement:** Add 1 to one's complement value

The question is, which one is popular in today's computers? Being even more specific, which are present in the Raspberry Pi? Three are used: two's complement represents signed integers in the ARM CPU while both sign/magnitude and bias are used in the floating point format. Table B.4 gives 8-bit binary examples where positive and negative 26_{10} are represented four ways. I've also included zero, including the rather unexpected negative zero case.

Decimal	+ 26	− 26	+ 0	− 0
Sign & Magnitude	00011010	10011010	00000000	10000000
One's Complement	00011010	11100101	00000000	11111111
Two's Complement	00011010	11100110	00000000	00000000
Biased	10011010	01100110	10000000	10000000

Table B.4: Comparison of +26, −26, +0, and −0 in four signed byte formats

Nine's complement

How can we subtract using an "adding machine"? This question was not new with electronic computers, but goes back to the days when accountants and human "computers" used mechanical adding machines. It involves converting the algebraic expression "A – B" to "A + (–B)" which transforms the question into how should we represent –B?

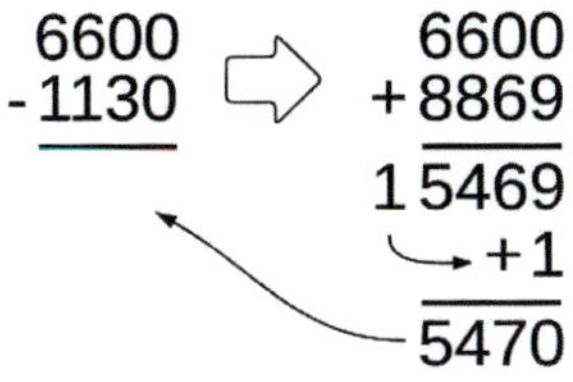

```
  6600  ⇨    6600
- 1130    + 8869
         ——————
          1 5469
            ↳ + 1
         ——————
          5470
```

Figure B.1: Nine's complement example of subtraction by addition

Accountants, working in base ten, could represent a negative number by subtracting each of its digits from nine (one less than the base). On the left, we see an example where the negative of 1130 is 8869 in nine's complement (each 8 comes from 9 – 1, the 6 comes from 9 – 3, and the 9 comes from 9 – 0).

Obviously, since we're adding, rather than subtracting, the result is larger than we want, but if you do the algebra, you'll notice that the correct answer can be achieved. Notice how the first sum in Figure B.0 had a "carry out" that did not fit in the number of columns we were using. If you add this carry in a second step as shown, the correct answer appears. If there is no carry, do not add it, and there will be a large number, but it is really a negative number.

One's complement

One's complement is the same as nine's complement except the base is now two: every digit is subtracted from 1, instead of 9. Actually, this technique works in any base. Do the algebra if you like to prove it. Because there's only two symbols in base 2, one's complement is achieved by simply inverting each bit as is shown in Figure B.2.

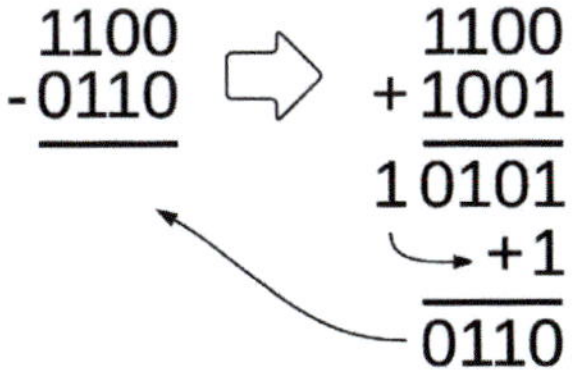

```
  1100  ⇨    1100
- 0110    + 1001
         ——————
          1 0101
            ↳ + 1
         ——————
          0110
```

Figure B.2: One's complement example of subtraction by addition

Just like in nine's complement a subtraction is converted into an addition. Here the negative of "0110" is calculated to be "1001" where the value in each column is calculated by subtracting it from one less than the base. Notice that it's still a two-step process where the carry out is added back to obtain the correct answer.

If you follow the above naming convention, you would think that two's complement involves numbers expressed in base 3. Actually, the expression "two's complement" refers to the technique that eliminates the second step during a subtraction.

Two's complement

In two's complement, the negative of a number is generated by adding one to the one's complement and ignoring any caries. For example, the negative of 0110 is 1001 + 1 = 1010.

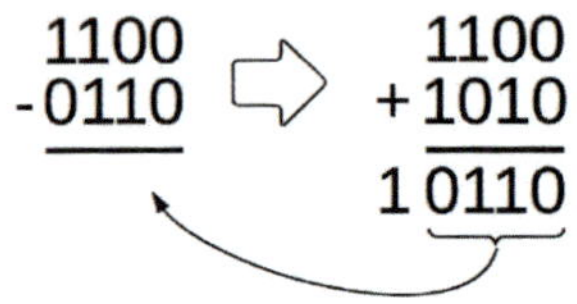

$$
\begin{array}{r} 1100 \\ -0110 \\ \hline \end{array}
\Rightarrow
\begin{array}{r} 1100 \\ +1010 \\ \hline 1\,0110 \end{array}
$$

Figure B.3: Two's complement example of subtraction by addition

Rather than adding the "carry out" as a second step, a 1-bit is added preemptively when the negative is generated. Then during the subtraction, the carry is just ignored, making two's complement subtractions twice as fast as one's complement subtractions.

Appendix C
Hexadecimal Numbers

To be precise, it's not the numbers that are hexadecimal, but the written representation of numbers. Hexadecimal is a compact form of binary representation where we have sixteen symbols {0,1,2,3,4,5,6,7,8,9,A,B,C,D,E,F} to represent numbers. If you're not familiar with binary representation, please read Appendix B before studying hexadecimal. If it wasn't for binary, there would be negligible need for hexadecimal in the computer industry.

A decimal number is really a short notation for a polynomial of powers of 10. For example: 137_{10} is $1{\times}10^2 + 3{\times}10^1 + 7{\times}10^0$ which is $100 + 30 + 7$. Likewise, a binary number is really a short notation for a polynomial of powers of 2. For example: 110101_2 is $1{\times}2^5 + 1{\times}2^4 + 0{\times}2^3 + 1{\times}2^2 + 0{\times}2^1 + 1{\times}2^0$. A hexadecimal number is really a short notation for a polynomial of powers of 16. For example: $5A732C_{16}$ is $5{\times}16^5 + 10{\times}16^4 + 7{\times}16^3 + 3{\times}16^2 + 2{\times}16^1 + 12{\times}16^0$ where A and C are digits representing values of 10 and 12, respectively.

Why Use Hexadecimal?

The simple answer is hexadecimal is compact, and it is very easy for us humans to convert between binary and hexadecimal. Consider the following:

1. Internally, almost all our computer systems are based in binary (see Lab 5 and Appendix B for an explanation).
2. Inputting and displaying numbers in the computer's natural binary notation is very efficient for the computer, but clumsy and inefficient for us humans. Who is comfortable reading and entering numbers like 100001101010010 or 1101101101101, and even much longer ones up to 64 bits in length?
3. Decimal is a rather compact form of representing numbers, and we are very comfortable with it because we use it in our daily lives. We can convert between decimal and binary by using successive divisions by ten. However, that is slow and cumbersome to do "in our heads." A division by sixteen is simply a four bit shift, but a division by ten cannot be achieved by shifting bits.
4. Do we humans actually need to use binary? As people working with computers at a detailed architectural level, we have to see the actual bits. We have to look at status words, IP addresses, instruction formats, and memory dumps.

Table C.1 shows counting from 0 to 17 in decimal, binary, hexadecimal, and octal. Notice how one hexadecimal digit fits exactly in four bits. Figure C.1 shows a binary number being "mapped" to hexadecimal digits, four bits at a time. starting from the right side.

base 10 10 symbols {0123456789}	base 2 2 symbols {01}	base 16 16 symbols {0123456789ABCDEF}	base 8 8 symbols {01234567}
0	0	0	0
1	1	1	1
2	10	2	2
3	11	3	3
4	100	4	4
5	101	5	5
6	110	6	6
7	111	7	7
8	1000	8	10
9	1001	9	11
10	1010	A	12
11	1011	B	13
12	1100	C	14
13	1101	D	15
14	1110	E	16
15	1111	F	17
16	10000	10	20
17	10001	11	21

Table C.1: Counting from 0 to 17 in four different bases

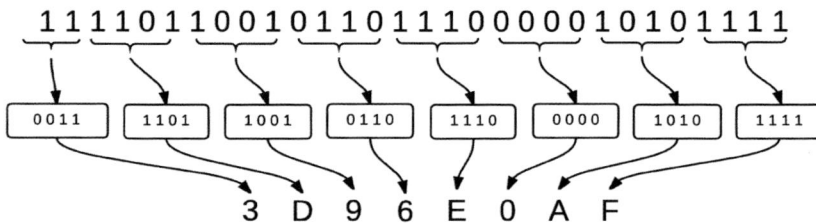

Figure C.1: Convert binary to hex, 4 bits at a time starting from the right (low order) side

Assembly Language Coding in Color

Appendix D
ASCII

Why ASCII? Why not Baudot, BCD, Display Code, Fieldata, Unicode, XS3, or any other character code?

What is a Character Code

Binary computers store and manipulate bits (binary digits). Numbers are represented by "groups of bits" as either integers or real numbers. That's fine for science and engineering applications, but what's stored in "groups of bits" for business applications, such as correspondence, reports, and mailing lists? How is this text data consisting of letters, digits, and punctuation represented by "groups of bits"? A character code is a set that assigns each text character to a unique number.

This was not so much of a problem 3000 years ago. Several of the ancient languages including Assyrian, Hebrew, and Greek were "computer ready," but our modern written languages, such as English, are not. In these ancient languages, every symbol used to compose words was also used to compose numbers. The symbols alpha and beta in Greek were assigned both sounds to form words as well as numeric values to write numbers. In English, letters and digits are separate (i.e., the letter "R" does not have a numeric value). This means there was no "standard" for storing text data as a series of numbers.

In the 1960s, several companies were manufacturing mainframe computer systems. They were competing for sales and were interested in locking customers into their unique designs rather than making computer data files and applications portable from one system to another. There were basically two problems with character codes in the 1960s:

- Each character was stored in a byte, but the number of bits composing a byte varied from system to system.
- Each character was assigned a unique numeric code, but each computer system had a different set of character code assignments..

Several mainframe computer systems had 6-bit bytes, which supported a set of 64 different characters. BCD, Display Code, Fieldata, and XS3 are examples of 6-bit codes. Each of these sets contained 26 upper case letters, 10 digits, and a few punctuation marks and control characters. In order to include lower case letters, IBM switched from a 6-bit code to an 8-bit EBCDIC code in the mid 1960s. The size of the byte determines how many different characters can be represented as listed below:

- 6 bits: 64 characters
- 7 bits: 128 characters
- 8 bits: 256 characters
- 16 bits: 65,536 characters

The second compatibility problem was that the unique assignments were inconsistent among the different character code sets and computer systems. It took a presidential decree to alleviate some of the inconsistencies. On March 11, 1968, President Johnson signed ASCII (American Standard Code for Information Interchange) into existence.

Character Code	Letter A	Digit 5	blank
IBM BCD	11	05	30
CDC Display Code	01	20	2D
Univac Fieldata	06	25	05
XS3	14	08	33
EBCDIC	C1	F5	40
ASCII	41	33	20
Unicode	41	33	20

Table D.1: Example of three characters expressed in various character codes (in hexadecimal)

The 7-bit ASCII code from 1968 was fine for the English language, but it could not even support all the characters used in French, Spanish, and other Latin languages. In 1985, character set ISO 8859 was defined as an 8-bit code with 256 character codes defined, where the first 128 are identical to 7-bit ASCII. The remaining 128 character codes were assigned to accent characters for the Latin languages and a variety of special symbols like copyright and trademark.

Hex Code	Symbol	Hex Code	Symbol	Hex Code	Symbol
30	0	40	@	50	P
31	1	41	A	51	Q
32	2	42	B	52	R
33	3	43	C	53	S
34	4	44	D	54	T
35	5	45	E	55	U
36	6	46	F	56	V
37	7	47	G	57	W
38	8	48	H	58	X
39	9	49	I	59	Y
3A	:	4A	J	5A	Z
3B	;	4B	K	5B	[
3C	<	4C	L	5C	\
3D	=	4D	M	5D	]
3E	>	4E	N	5E	^
3F	?	4F	O	5F	_

Table D.2: ASCII and ISO codes in hexadecimal

Hex Code	Symbol	Hex Code	Symbol	Hex Code	Symbol
60	`	70	p		
61	a	71	q		
62	b	72	r		
63	c	73	s		
64	d	74	t		
65	e	75	u		
66	f	76	v		
67	g	77	w		
68	h	78	x		
69	i	79	y		
6A	j	7A	z		
6B	k	7B	{		
6C	l	7C	|		
6D	m	7D	}		
6E	n	7E	~		
6F	o	7F			

Table D.3: ASCII and ISO codes in hexadecimal

What about those written languages like Hebrew and Greek that were "computer ready" thousands of years ago? Were they still computer ready in 1968 when ASCII was defined? They were by themselves, but to include them alongside ASCII and ISO 8895, a new character set has been defined: Unicode. Casually speaking, Unicode is considered to be a 16-bit code supporting 65,536 different character code symbols, enough to encompass all the written symbols composing thousands of different languages. The first 128 characters of Unicode are the same as the ASCII character set.

Appendix E
Text Editors

Editing is the first step in the vicious cycle of edit-compile-link-execute used to test and debug software programs. A "word processor" program cannot be used to generate or update the assembler source code because it inserts many hidden commands for changing fonts, formatting pages, and including images that would not be meaningful to the assembler. Appendix E provides a brief introduction to three text editors included in the Raspian Linux distribution that are compatible with editing assembly language source code files.

Program Source Code

Assembly language source code files have a simple structure consisting of the following ASCII characters:

1. **"Printable" Characters:** A, B, C, ... 1, 2, 3, ..., #, !, [,], ... See Appendix D for a full list. If the hash symbol (#, "pound sign") is missing, see Appendix A for suggestions for Linux system configuration.
2. **Line Feed "control character":** Hexadecimal code 0x0A terminates each line.
3. **Horizontal Tab "control character":** Hexadecimal code 0x09 separates each column. One or more blanks would work as well, but tabs automatically form columns.
4. **No line numbers:** Although line numbers appear on listings and error diagnostics, they're not physically in the file. The text editors can count lines and display that count if the user chooses.

```
          .global    _start      @ Indicate _start is global for linker
_start:   mov        R0,#78      @ Move a decimal 78 value into register R0
          mov        R7,#1       @ Move a decimal 1 integer value into register R7
          svc        0           @ Perform Service Call to Linux
          .end
```

Listing E.1: Sample source code for assembly language program

Leafpad Editor

Most of my students prefer to use the Leafpad editor and like its features due to its similarity to PC-based text editors. Students usually keep the following two windows constantly open and switch back and forth between them:

1. Leafpad full screen editor for constructing the source code
2. LXTerminal (Lightweight X Terminal emulator) for command lines

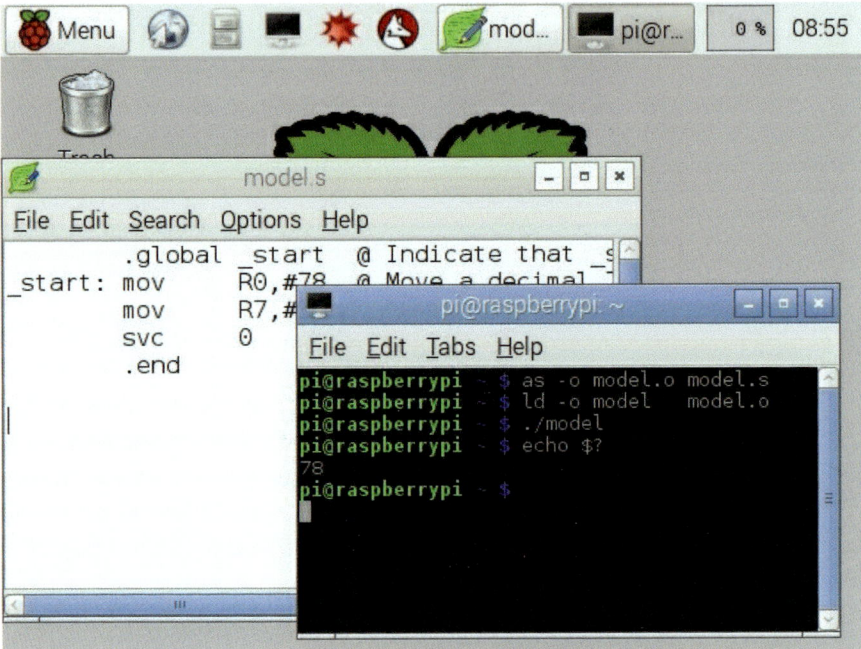

Figure E.1: Two windows open: one for editing and one for testing

The Leafpad editor is a "simple text editor" that can be opened from the accessories pull-down menu as show in Figure E.2. It can also be started by double clicking on the assembly language source code file displayed in the GUI file explorer.

Figure E.2: LXTerminal and Leafpad in pull-down menu

Once open, the user can move around the screen with either the mouse or arrow keys. Editing is basically done by inserting new text at the current cursor position or replacing ("keying over") text at the current cursor position. The keyboard "Insert" key enables toggling between insert and replace mode.

As shown in Figure E.3, commonly used search and edit functions are accessed through pull-down menus as well as control keys.

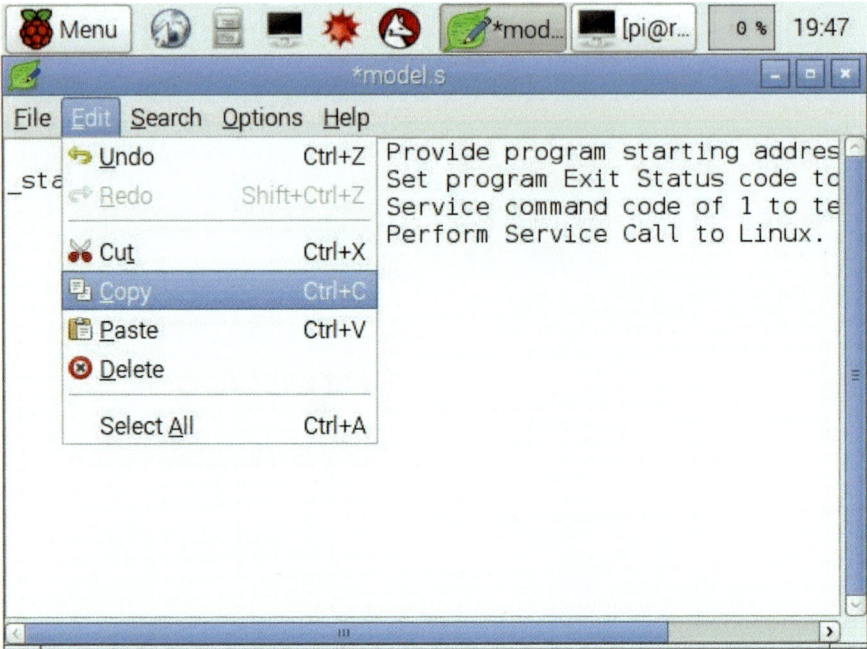

Figure E.3: Leafpad has pull-down menus and control-key commands.

Exiting the editor is done with either the control-q key or by "x-ing" out of the window. Most students don't exit, but use the control-s to save the file updates and then switch to the command window to assemble, link, and debug. After testing their updates, the students then return to the open editor window and continue modifying their programs.

Nano Editor

Many of my students prefer to work entirely in command line mode using an editor such as nano, vi, vim, or emacs. Of these, nano is by far the easiest one to begin using. It is started by entering "nano model.s" on the command line to edit a file named model.s.

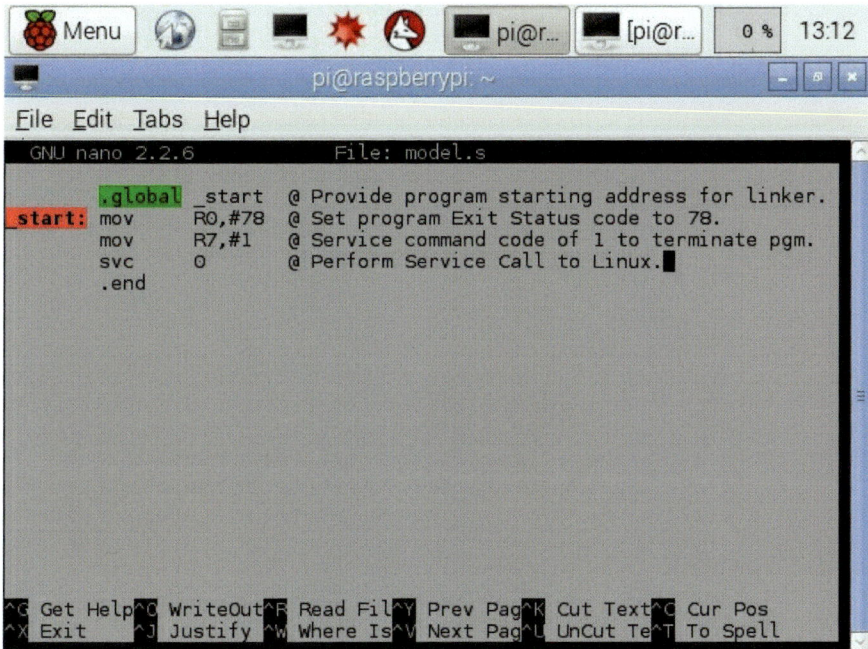

Figure E.4: Nano editor with first program displayed.

Several commands are available and each is invoked by holding down the control-key along with one of the letters listed on the bottom of the editing window as displayed in Figure E.4 and Table E.1.

^G Get Help	^O WriteOut	^R Read File	^Y Prev Page	^K Cut Text	^C Cur Pos
^X Exit	^J Justify	^W Where Is	^V Next Page	^U UnCut Text	^T To Spell

Table E.1: Nano control commands

The control-G "Get Help" command provides background on the nano editor and describes its editing commands as shown in Figure E.4. Some of the commands, such as control-J to justify text, are not very useful for an assembly language program. The copy-paste capability using control-K and control-U is present, but limited to one line of text at a time.

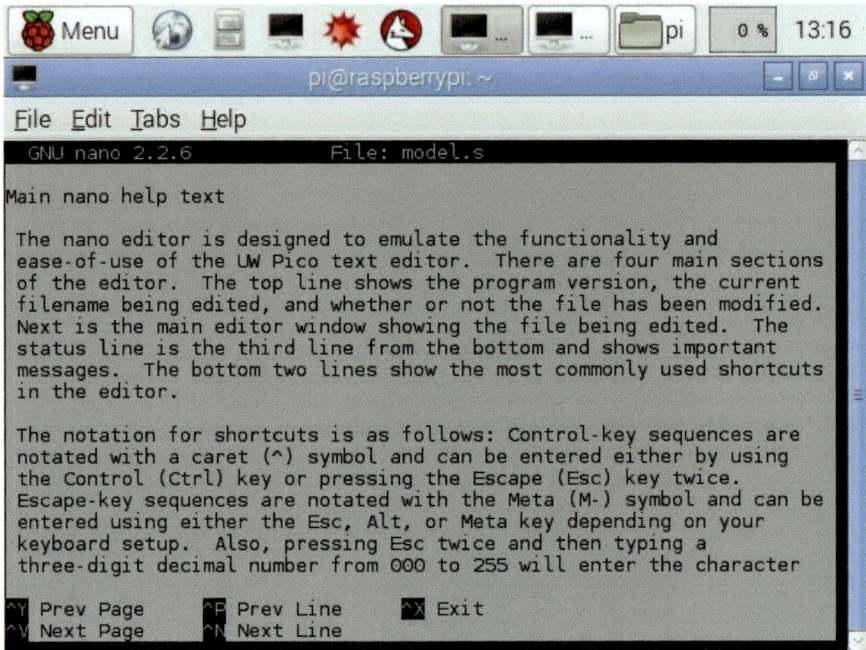

Figure E.5: Nano editor Help screen (control G)

Exiting from the nano editor is done using a control-X. If any updating was performed, the following prompt will appear. After answering "Y," a second prompt will appear to see if the file name to be written should be changed.

- Save modified buffer (ANSWERING "No" WILL DESTROY CHANGES) ?
- File Name to Write [DOS Format]: model.s

vi Editor

The vi editor is typically used by students who already have some experience with Linux or Unix. This will be an extremely brief introduction to vi. Once you get a little experience with it, please check the many Internet sites for many more features you might find useful.

The vi editor is started by entering "vi model.s" on the command line to edit a file named model.s. This editor has two modes: insert and command. Insert mode is similar to the full screen mode of nano and Leafpad where editing takes place by keying in new text at the current cursor location. The backspace key will delete the character to its left, and the delete key will delete the character at or to the right of the cursor. The keyboard "Insert" key will toggle between inserting and replacing ("key over") characters at the current cursor position.

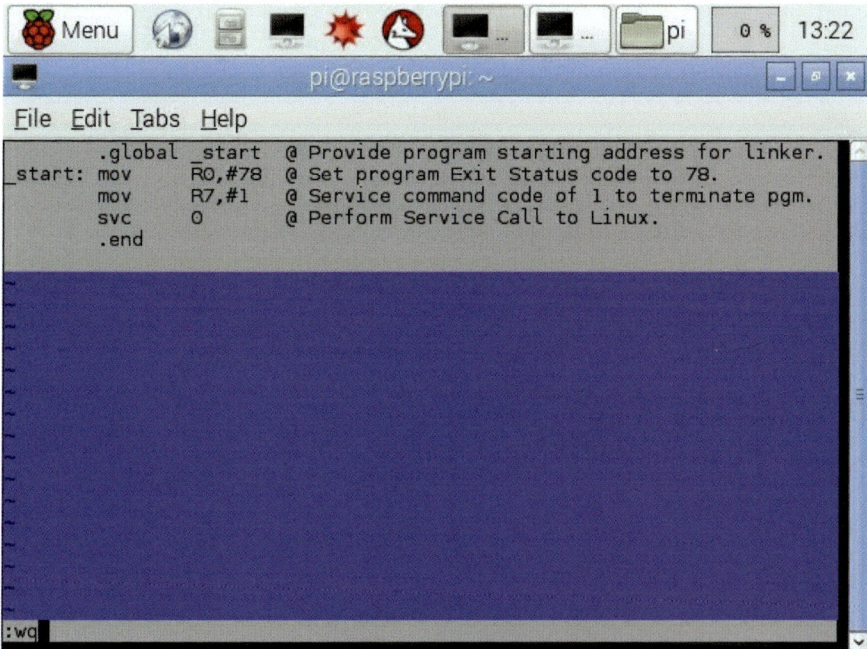

Figure E.6: vi editor screen with "wq" exit command displayed.

Command mode is entered by keying in the ESC key while in insert mode. One group of commands is initiated by keying in a colon character which brings the cursor down to a blank command line on the bottom of the screen. As shown in Figure E.6, the vi editor is typically exited while in command mode by entering one of the following responses to the "colon" command:

- :wq: Save updates and exit.

- :q!: Exit and ignore any changes.

Insert mode is entered when vi starts, and insert mode can be reentered from command mode by entering one of the following commands:

- i: Insert before current cursor, I: Insert at beginning of current line.
- a: Inset After current cursor, A: Append at end of current line
- o: Open a new line after current line, O: Open a new line before current line.
- cc: Delete current line and open new one in its place.
- R: Enter replace mode (i.e., "key over") at current cursor.

While in command mode, the cursor can be moved using the arrow, page-up, and page-down keys. It can also be moved using one of the following:

- G: Go to the end of the file. If preceded by a number, such as "7G" the cursor will go to beginning of line 7.
- /: Search forward in the file for the string (cursor temporarily drops to bottom of screen to enter search string terminated by the "enter" key).
- ?: Search backward (toward beginning of file) for string.
- n: Forward search using same string from previous search.
- N: Backward search using same string from previous search.

Single characters and lines can be deleted by entering the following keys. Preceding the commands with a number will delete multiple characters or lines.

- r: Replace one character (i.e., type over) at current cursor.
- x: Delete one character to the right of current cursor position.
- X: Delete one character to the left of cursor.
- D Delete to the end of the line.
- dd Delete current line (3dd deletes 3 lines).

Lines of text can be copied (yanked) into a buffer and later pasted. By preceding the following commands with a quote (") and a letter name, multiple unique buffers are available. For example, "a3yy copies 3 lines to buffer "a" which can be pasted with "ap.

- yy: Yank the current line (i.e., copy text into a temporary buffer).
- p: Put (or paste) saved buffer contents after the line of current cursor.
- P: Put saved buffer contents before the current line.

The search and replace command is entered following a colon. Its general format is %s/str1/str2/gc where occurrences of str1 will be replaced by str2. If the % is omitted, only the current line is searched, and if the g is omitted, only the first occurrence will be replaced. If the c is included, then all substitutions will be prompted for a confirmation.

Appendix F
List of Instructions

Appendix F provides a list of ARM and NEON instructions and assembler directives used in this book. The first column in each of the following tables contains a three number field indicating the chapter, listing number, and text line number where the instruction is used first. For example, 3.5.27 indicates the instruction is on line 27 of Listing 5 in Chapter 3.

5.1.18.	add	R1,R5	@ [R1] = [R1] + [R5]
3.5.27.	add	R3,R1,#1	@ [R3] = [R1] + 1
7.2.33.	addlt	R3,R5	@ If Z-flag=0 and N-flag=1, then do add.
5.1.17.	and	R1,#1	@ [R1] = [R1] AND 0b00000001
6.4.16.	and	R1,R4,R3,LSR R6	@ [R1] = [R4] AND ([R3] >> [R6])
3.3.29.	bgt	_start	@ If Z-flag=0 and N-flag=1, then branch..
4.1.26.	bl	v_asc1	@ Branch/Link (call subroutine).
4.1.60.	bx	LR	@ Branch exchange (return from subroutine).
3.3.28.	cmp	R2,#1	@ Set CPSR flags as if SUBS was performed.
7.5.31.	eor	R8,R8,R12	@ [R8] = [R8] XOR [R12]
3.1.5.	ldr	R1,=msg	@ [R1] = memory address of label "msg:"
5.1.9.	ldrb	R3,[R1]	@ Load byte from memory, bits 8-31 get zero.
7.2.26.	ldrb	R5,[R4],#-1	@ Load byte and post-increment R4
7.10.30.	ldmia	R1,{R8-R11}	@ Load multiple register from memory address [R1]
5.1.16.	lsr	R1,R6	@ [R1] = [R1] >> [R6]
2.1.2.	mov	R0,#78	@ [R0] = 78
7.2.19.	mul	R2,R0	@ [R2] = [R2] × [R0]
7.5.38.	orr	R8,R8,R12	@ [R8] = [R8] OR [R12]
4.1.59.	pop	{R0,R2,R7}	@ Restore registers saved on stack.
4.1.54.	push	{R0,R2,R7}	@ Save contents of registers in stack memory.
7.10.35.	stmia	R1,{R8-R11}	@ Store multiple registers to memory at [R1].
7.2.18.	strb	R2,[R4,#1]!	@ Increment R4 and store bits 0-7 from R2.
3.5.31.	subs	R4,#1	@ [R4] = [R4] - 1, then set CPSR flags
2.1.4.	svc	0	@ Issue Linux command

Listing F.1: Program location for first appearance of ARM instruction

8.3.32.	vadd.u8	D1,D1,D1	@ [D1] = [D1] + [D1], using eight 8-bit lanes.
8.1.37.	veor	Q0,Q0,Q1	@ Exclusive OR of 128 bit registers
8.1.32.	vldm	R1,{Q0}	@ Load 128-bit Q0 from memory at [R1]
8.1.45.	vorr	Q0,Q0,Q1	@ Inclusive OR of 128-bit registers, Q0, Q1
8.1.39.	vstm	R1,{Q0}	@ Store 128-bit register into 16 bytes of memory.
8.6.13.	vst1.8	{D0−D2},[R1]	@ Store as 1 "element" of 8 bits each
8.6.16.	vst3.8	{D0−D2},[R1]	@ Store as 3 "elements" of 8 bits each
8.6.19.	vst3.16	{D0−D2},[R1]	@ Store as 3 "elements" of 16 bits each
8.6.22.	vst3.32	{D0−D2},[R1]	@ Store as 3 "elements" of 32 bits each

Listing F.2: Program location for first appearance of NEON instruction

List of first use of assembler directives			
3.1.18.	.ascii	"Hello World\n"	@ ASCII string, 1 character per byte
7.2.47.	.byte	1	@ Initialize byte in memory.
3.1.17.	.data		@ Begin "data" section of memory
3.2.24.	.ds	10	@ Reserve 10 16-bit words of memory
2.1.5.	.end		@ End of source code file
4.2.13.	.endm		@ End of macro definition
2.1.1.	.global	_start:	@ Define address for linker
4.2.7.	.macro	disp sub, tail	@ Begin macro definition
4.1.46.	.text		@ Begin "program" section of memory
7.5.52.	.word	0x20202020	@ Initialize word in memory.

Listing F.3: Program location for first appearance of assembler directive

Not all ARM and NEON instructions nor assembler directives are represented in this book. There are many very good technical reference manuals on these processors available on the Internet that provide tables of all possible instructions and directives.

Appendix G
Linux Service Calls

One of the main responsibilities of an operating system, such as Linux, is to provide services for application programs. A large portion of these services involves reading and writing peripheral devices (display monitor, keyboard, mouse, network, etc.) and disk files (real spinning disks as well as solid-state memory devices). The calling program must provide Linux with the details of what is to be performed:

1. What is to be done (register R7)
2. Which device is to written or read (register R0)
3. Where the data buffer is in the program's memory (register R1)
4. How much data is to be written or read (register R2)

	List of Linux service calls introduced in Labs
1	Terminate the program.
3	Read bytes from device into memory buffer
4	Write array of bytes to device from memory buffer

Service 1: Terminate program

Application programs start when Linux gives them control at the "_start" label, and when a program chooses to quit, it will return control back to Linux using a service call (SVC 0 instruction).

```
mov    R0,#0    @ Exit status code in register R0
mov    R7,#1    @ Linux service code 1 put into register R7.
svc    0        @ Perform service call to Linux
```

Listing G.1: Example from Chapter 2 to quit program

Service 3: Read data from I/O device into memory buffer

Many custom devices and disk files can be supported, but there are a few device names that have become standard and appear in all Linux and Unix systems. The device *stdin* refers to the standard character input stream that by default is the keyboard, but can be redirected to an alternate device or file. This service call returns register R0 with the number of bytes that were read into the buffer. This byte count may be less than the value provided in register R2, but will not be more.

```
ldr    R1,=msg     @ Memory address to receive input
mov    R0,#0       @ Stdin: Standard input (usually keyboard)
mov    R7,#3       @ Linux command code to read
mov    R2,#20      @ Maximum length to receive
svc    0           @ Issue command to read.
```

Listing G.2: Example from Chapter 3 to read characters from keyboard

Service 4: Write data from memory buffer to I/O device

A second standard device name is *stdout* which by default is the display monitor, but can be redirected to an alternate device or file.

```
ldr    R1,=msg     @ Load pointer to message.
mov    R2,#12      @ Number of characters in message
mov    R0,#1       @ Code for stdout (usually the monitor)
mov    R7,#4       @ Linux service command code to write
svc    0           @ Call Linux command.
```

Listing G.3: Example from Chapter 3 to write to display monitor

Linux obviously provides many more services than what is listed above. Tables containing over one hundred service codes can easily be found on the Internet. Note: Some of the codes and their responses vary depending on the version of Linux being used.

Appendix H
C Programming

Assembly language programs target specific CPU architectures. The C programming language was developed at AT&T Bell Laboratories as a "portable" alternative to assembly language for developing software such as operating systems that needed low-level access to the hardware.

Although almost all of the embedded systems that I have programmed consist of a combination of assembly language with a higher level language like C, I wanted this book to be focused 100% on assembly language. However, I do want to provide a brief clue as to how to call an assembly language subroutine from a C program.

There are basically two techniques used to pass a variable's data in arguments to a subroutine:

- Pass by value: The value of a variable is passed in a register or on the stack, and the subroutine has no access to the source variable itself.
- Pass by reference: The memory address of a variable is passed, and the subroutine can actually update the variable in the calling routine's data area.

Listing H.1 contains a very short C main program in file "model.c" that calls two assembly language routines that calculate the sum of an array of 32-bit integers:

- thesum: Subroutine that returns the sum to a reference argument
- fcnsum: Function that returns the sum as the return value of the function

```
1.          #include <stdio.h>
2.          #include <stdlib.h>
3.
4.          int main() {
5.              int count = 3, totalA, totalB, tstdat[] = {11, 45, 70};
6.              thesum (&totalA, tstdat, 3);
7.              totalB = fcnsum (tstdat, count);
8.              printf ("Sum from subroutine = %d\n", totalA);
9.              printf ("Sum from function = %d\n", totalB);
10.             return 0;
11.         }
```

Listing H.1: Main C program calling a subroutine and a function

Listing H.2 provides file "sum.s" that contains both the function and subroutine called by the C main program. Notice that the arguments appear very similar to what we have been using in all the chapters.

```
 1.        .global    thesum     @ Subroutine entry address to linker
 2.        .global    fcnsum     @ Function entry address to linker
 3.
 4. @      Subroutine thesum adds a variable number of integers.
 5. @                 R0: Memory address of variable to receive the sum.
 6. @                 R1: Memory address of array of integer values
 7. @                 R2: Number of integers in the array
 8. @                 LR: Contains the return address
 9. @                 Registers R1 through R3 will be not saved.
10.
11. thesum:  ldr     R3,[R1],#4 @ Load first value.
12.          subs    R2,#1      @ Decrement number of integers.
13.          ble     retsub     @ Return with just one value.
14.          push    {R4}       @ R4 contents must be preserved.
15. thelp:   ldr     R4,[R1],#4 @ Load next interger in list.
16.          add     R3,R4      @ Add it to the running total.
17.          subs    R2,#1      @ Number of integers still to add.
18.          bne     thelp      @ Continue with next integer
19.          pop     {R4}
20. retsub:  str     R3,[R0]    @ Return sum to calling program
21.          bx      LR         @ Return to calling program
22.
23. @      Function fcnsum adds a variable number of integers.
24. @                 R0: Memory address of array of integer values
25. @                 R1: Number of integers in the array
26. @                 LR: Contains the return address
27. @                 R0: Return calculated sum to calling program.
28. @                 Registers R0 through R3 will be not saved.
29.
30. fcnsum:  ldr     R3,[R0],#4 @ Load first value.
31.          subs    R1,#1      @ Decrement number of integers.
32.          ble     retfcn     @ Return with just one value.
33. fcnlp:   ldr     R2,[R0],#4 @ Load next interger in list.
34.          add     R3,R2      @ Add it to the running total.
35.          subs    R1,#1      @ Number of integers still to add.
36.          bne     fcnlp      @ Continue with next integer
37. retfcn:  mov     R0,R3      @ Return sum to calling program
38.          bx      LR         @ Return to calling program
39.          .end
```

Listing H.2: Assembly language subroutine and function called by C main program

Use the "gcc" command to compile the C main program and assembly language subprograms as seen on the first line in Listing H.3. This one command line will also link this simple program. The second line of Listing H.3 obviously runs the program, and the final two lines are the output from the program.

```
~$ gcc  -o  model  model.c  sum.s
~$ ./model
Sum from subroutine = 126
Sum from function = 126
```

Listing H.3: Compile/link, execute, and two lines of output

Generally speaking, the difference between a function and a subroutine is a function returns a value and a subroutine does not. However, as seen in this example, a subroutine can return one or more values through arguments "passed by reference." In situations where only one value is returned, it is advisable to only use a function because 1) it hides the location of the actual data, 2) it is more efficient, and 3) it is expected to be done (self documenting).

- Arguments are passed in registers R0 through R3. If there are more than four arguments, those are pushed onto the stack.
- The calling program does not expect the contents in registers R0 through R3 to be preserved.
- A function returns its value in register R0.
- The Link Register (LR) contains the return address.
- Arrays are passed by reference.
- Constants and single variables are passed by value.
- A single variable can be passed by reference if preceded by an ampersand.

Arguments	Pass by __	Location
thesum (&totalA, tstdat, 3); // a subroutine		
&totalA	Reference	[R0]
tstdat	Reference	[R1]
3	Value	R2
totalB = fcnsum (tstdat, count); // a function		
tstdat	Reference	[R0]
count	Value	R1
totalB	Value	R0

Table H.1: Subroutine and function arguments in example program

H: C Programming

AAPCS Subroutine Interface

The *Procedure Call Standard for the ARM Architecture (AAPCS)* properly describes what I have just briefly introduced. This standard, which is part of the *Application Binary Interface (ABI) for the ARM Architecture*, is not only used for C, but can be used for other languages as well. Very similar techniques have been available on other architectures for decades.

Java, C++, C#

The C++ language is an enhancement to C to incorporate some object oriented programming features. C++ is not a pure object oriented language like Smalltalk, but a hybrid. Calling assembly language subroutines from C++ is possible, but there are more types of arguments possible. I won't describe C++ here as most embedded systems use "straight" C rather than C++.

Although the original incentive for developing the Java language was to develop embedded systems, it has expanded to encompass much of the computer industry. Java source code, which looks very similar to that of C++, is compiled into an intermediate "byte code" object code rather than true CPU-specific machine code instructions. This byte code is then run interpretively on top of a "Java virtual machine." It is interesting to note that there is another coprocessor within the Raspberry Pi that facilitates the running of the "Java virtual machine."

C# is one of Microsoft's *.net* programming languages and has a syntax similar to C++, but compiles into an "assembly" intermediate object code that runs on top of Microsoft's "framework" which is similar to a virtual machine. Neither Java nor any of the .net languages interfaces as easily with native assembly language as does C.

Assembly Language Coding in Color

Index